The

Prepper's Long-Term
SURVIVAL BIBLE

8 in 1

The Ultimate Life-Savings Strategies for Self-Sufficient, Off-Grid Shelter, and Home-defense to Survive Everywhere During any Disaster

---

Table of Contents

INTRODUCTION

The world that we live in is unpredictable. It's full of hazards that can develop in a moment's notice. I don't mean to paint a grim picture, but catastrophic weather, shocking accidents, and terrifying acts are part of our reality. Don't believe me? Just turn on the world news for a week! One day is likely enough.

This guide will provide you with valuable knowledge that will allow you to properly confront these situations when they arise. My book lays out simple guidance and procedures that can be used by people of all backgrounds and skill levels—young and old alike.

Since childhood, I have studied and implemented survival techniques into my life by trial and error. Throughout my adult life, I have been involved with a group of close friends who have taken any survival information we could find and actually tested it in the field. I have also spent time in the military serving as a U.S. Army Airborne Ranger. As a soldier, fighting in multiple combat deployments, I learned a great deal concerning this topic. My years of experience have taken me into every one of earth's climate zones (except the arctic), but as a long-time resident of Wisconsin, I am no stranger to the extreme cold either. That being said, you do not need a list of credentials or years of practice to benefit from this book.

By incorporating these tips and basic skills you will become mentally stronger, more resourceful, and better prepared for potentially hazardous situations. Before long, you will find that much of what you learn here is going to find its way into your everyday life and it will come through paths that you never expected. Get used to saying, I'm glad I was ready for that!

Often, we are not talking about life and death here. There is a good chance that you will frequently use these skills to help others who were not prepared. I am not a doctor, but there have been a great many times that a bit of knowledge and some common medical supplies have come into play.

Once, two of my survival companions and I were on a two-week canoe trip into a remote wilderness area in Northern Minnesota and Canada called the Boundary Waters. It is a place of profound beauty that is virtually untouched by civilization. While at camp one afternoon, another canoe came over to us in need of help. One of the guys in their group had seriously cut his hand while preparing food and they could not get the bleeding to stop. The simple med kit they brought only had a few small bandages.

They were not prepared. I was able to provide them with some crucial knowledge and coagulation powder to stop the bleeding. With heavy bandage and gauze, he was able to properly wrap the wound. Would that guy have died? I am quite certain that he would have made it, but they were a few days from civilization and that is a long time to bleed! The point is that with a bit of know-how and the right supplies, I was able to help make a difference.

I can honestly guarantee that the things you learn in this book will allow you to make a difference too. There is a profound satisfaction that comes with being able to help another. That canoer was someone that I didn't know and will never see again. Think about your friends and family. How deeply do you care about them? I promise that one day when you least expect it, you WILL need this information.

Don't be the one who says it won't happen to me. It's a trap for the weak! Don't be the one who is afraid and helpless when things get ugly or you and your loved ones are in need. The regret will leave you numb with emptiness. Be the one who others look to because you have the solution. Be the one who has what is needed when the time comes. Be the one who will confidently take action that is reinforced with the proper knowledge. You CAN be the one who is able to make the difference!

Through countless experiences, this knowledge has proven itself time and time again. Some of this wisdom, simple though it may be, has remained valid for thousands of years. Other portions will incorporate the use of modern advancements. Each chapter of Simple Survival will bring you closer to being prepared for the worst. The pieces are here. Now, it's time to pick up what you've been missing.

Book 1:

Survival & Disaster

WHY SURVIVAL?

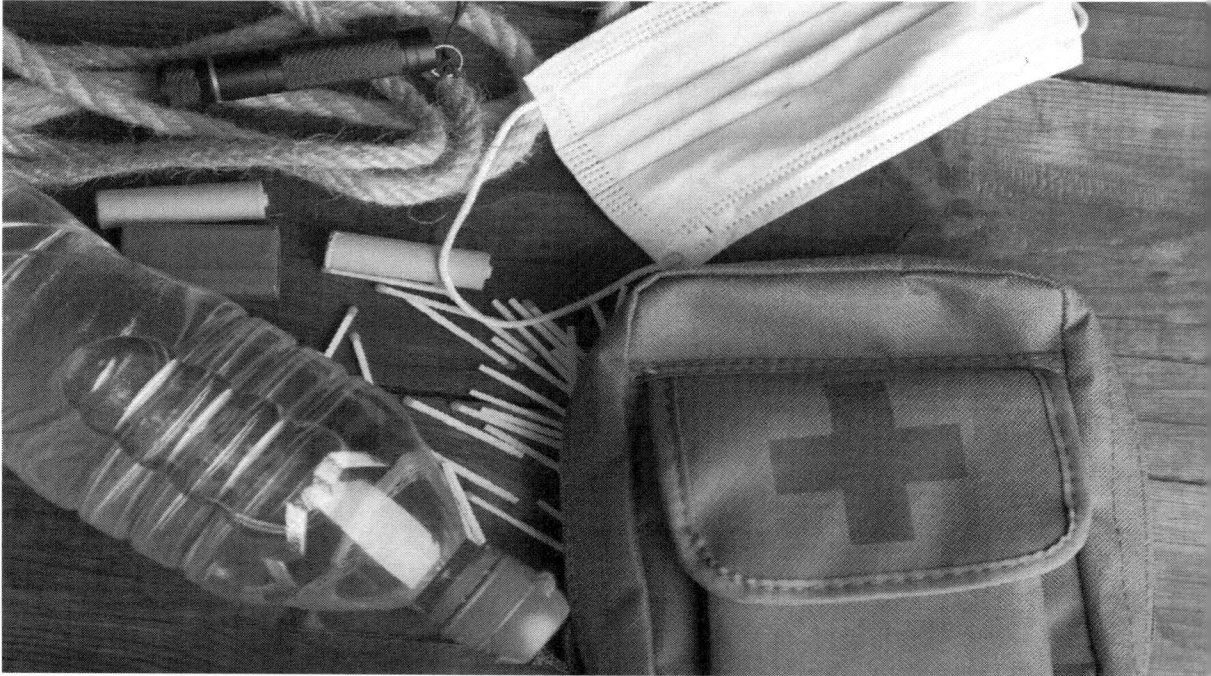

Survival skills are for everyone. It is something that has followed humanity since the dawn of time. Unfortunately, as years passed, the ease of modern convenience and technology has taken us farther and farther away from those critical skills. It has left us with a civilization that is no longer self-reliant. Most of our population is unknowing and ill-prepared.

Losing these skills does not mean that we no longer need them. It does not mean that we are no longer faced with problems, emergencies, and natural disasters. It means that when these situations arise, the greater majority will be blindsided and succumb to the detrimental effects of what has taken place.

More often than not, we do not have the power to prevent every negative circumstance. That is reality. What we do have is the ability to equip ourselves mentally and physically with the proper tools to deal with those circumstances when they are encountered.

We can see evidence of people suffering every day because of forgotten knowledge and the loss of abilities which allow us to persevere while under duress. Tragedy is still commonplace across the globe. The indicators show that the struggle is widespread and often far more intense than it should be.

This is simply due to one major factor. The populace just does not know what to do when disaster strikes. The scary thing is that we watch these things happening to people every day on the television. We are aware of the potential risk. We know that it is commonplace. The obvious is laid out before us and yet for some reason many choose to put blinders on. This is a mistake.

In the military, we identify potential dangers with information and observation. Once those dangers are clear, we gather knowledge that can help us adapt. We train ourselves on the ways to deal with them and acquire the equipment that will be necessary for these situations. Why should it be any different for a civilian?

Natural disasters happen on every part of Earth without exception. Every time, the majority of people are not prepared.

In recent years, natural disasters have displaced an average of twenty-five million people from their homes each year. That number almost doubles if you factor in the people who are affected by conflict zones. Amidst all of this, most people will do little to ensure their safety. It is just not clear why this is so. It seems unreasonable.

WHY SURVIVALIST SKILLS ARE MORE IMPORTANT THAN STUFF

As the world becomes more and more compact, its predictability is getting worse and worse. As conflicts escalate and disasters strike, governments can't be relied on to help us. We must develop the skills to get by with or without them:

- Choosing when to fight and when not to fight
- When it's better not to resist
- Living in a climate of scarcity
- Adapting and innovating under pressure
- Doing more with less

That's why these skills are so important. They're some of the most fundamental human qualities there are—survivalist skills that allow people under any conditions, anywhere in the world, to live well without reliance on anyone else.

The skills I'm talking about are these:

- Self-reliance
- Preparedness
- Social intelligence
- Conviction

- Resilience

They could be called the survivalist B vitamins. They're essential for survival under any circumstances, anywhere in the world, and they're necessary for not just physical survival but also mental and emotional survival. All five of them—no matter what disasters come your way—you can't live without them. You need them to live with what we call civilization, although it's not civilization by any standards you have been taught or perhaps even recognize as such.

The skills are especially crucial now because disaster is becoming global, and we're moving toward a world that's highly dependent on technology. They're fundamental to you, your family, friends and neighbors, coworkers and colleagues in your local community, or even senior management at your company. But these skills aren't just important for people who live in tough times:

These five core survivalist skills are also essential for anyone who may be called upon to help others survive—whether it be as a first responder or a humanitarian aid worker. I'm not talking about simply knowing these skills—I'm talking about actually using them in catastrophic situations. The person who's prepared and who uses these skills will survive better than the person who isn't.

I've talked with a few first responders, aid workers, and people from nonprofits that regularly find themselves on the scene of disasters—even though they weren't prepared—and they'll tell you that they wished they had prepared for the disaster beforehand so that they could help more people. Sometimes the first thing that's cut is money for emergency response training, and it's usually because there are people in charge who don't understand why training is important or how it helps people in dire circumstances. Training helps people in dire circumstances because it gives them the skills to help themselves and others survive.

Disasters hit, people panic, and governments seem incapable of responding—if they even bother to respond at all. This is why survivalist skills are more important than stuff.

When we can really use help from outside sources, we get less help than ever before. We've designed disaster relief systems that rely on other people taking care of us, but what happens when they can't? What happens when the nature of disasters has changed from isolated incidents into frequent events that overmatch the ability of responders at all levels? The answer is clear: you're totally on your own.

In the United States, three million households have no access to a car and live more than a mile away from the nearest supermarket. They are also dependent on public transit because they can't afford to own a car. At least one in twelve people in large urban areas—including New York City, Los Angeles, and Detroit—live below the poverty line, which means that they have limited or no access to food at all. In fact, 45 percent of Americans can't survive for more than two weeks without a job—what do you think would happen if they lost their job? If you're like most Americans, your answer is probably "add another month" or maybe "receive some government assistance."

But in a disaster, the government can't always come through—they might not even be around to respond or they may be overwhelmed by so many people in need. It's because of this that you have to make sure that you're prepared no matter what happens.

In the United States, your access to food is highly dependent on your income and employment status. If you're employed and middle class—if you have a home, some savings, and disposable income—then you can usually get what you need. If not, then it's much harder.

I remember speaking with a family in Sicily who were victims of the Mount Etna eruption in 2002. They lost their entire farm and they had no insurance. The family was originally from Egypt but moved to Sicily during World War II and were now living in a tent for a year on the government's dime.

The husband was also dying from cancer—they couldn't access the drugs he desperately needed without paying for them out of pocket, which ate up most of their meager savings. They couldn't buy food at all because they had no income. But even if they could have bought food, the closest market was miles away, and there were no shops closer than that because of how spread out people live on the island. I remember thinking how lucky I was to have grown up in the United States, even though it was hardly "lucky" to grow up with a roof over my head and food on the table.

This family, along with most of Sicily, was dependent on the government for everything that they needed—including food—but they could not rely on the government to guarantee their survival. That safety net is gone for many people both here and abroad.

While it's important to have a well-stocked pantry, that's not enough. You need extra food stashed away in case you can't access your regular stockpile. You need water stored in an offsite location (or multiple locations). You need to know that there are medicines that you have on hand in case of an emergency—and you also need to know how to use them. You need a safe place, away from the hazards of your home, for your important documents, records, family photos, and other mementos. You need a way to escape the area if necessary.

You also need insurance against things like earthquakes and floods. Earthquake insurance is usually more expensive than regular insurance, but it's worth it—I cannot tell you how many times I've had a client whose home was severely damaged because they were uninsured after an earthquake or other disaster.

We've all heard the stories of people in the US who "manage" by living off of rice and beans. Few of us have to do that ourselves because we have basic needs covered. But those who do—especially those living in the developing world, or among families with limited resources—live under constant threat.

I'm busy enough making sure that my family is well adapted for any foreseeable situation. But I'm not alone; there are others out there doing it as well. This article is part of a series on preparedness, but it's only one piece of a much larger puzzle.

I've been in the preparedness community for a while. I have also had enough time to know that many people claim to be prepared, but in fact, they have not. They haven't really thought it through. They don't have a plan, and they haven't taken any steps to make sure that they're prepared for a crisis of any kind.

The problem is that their declarations of readiness mean nothing because they've never done anything to prove it. It's like saying you're going on an adventure, but you haven't taken even the most basic steps toward preparing for your trip. They haven't packed their backpack, and they haven't practiced their survival skills with a knife, compass, map, and the ability to communicate in the wild.

But what about those who are doing it? How did they prepare, and in what ways have they actually been prepared? I decided to take a closer look into what some of them have done to find out more.

To do this, I reached out to an array of preppers—those who are prepared for anything—and asked them questions about how they've prepared for whatever calamity has ever befallen them. Or would befall them.

One prepper said he had a "shelter plan" in place *every year*. That's right, he knows exactly where he will live—and with whom—five years from now. He also told me that he isn't worried about wind turbines or solar panels ruining his home, because he has sirens and warning klaxons mounted on every square inch of his property.

His plan was for him, his wife, and his two daughters (no pets) to survive in the event of a disaster. He mentioned that he had his water filtered through three layers of plastic and that he sleeps on a thermal pad to keep himself warm and cozy at night. He also told me that he's stocked up on food and emergency drinking water so that if anything would happen to the power grid, he could survive for months underground. He's used blue lights at home to disorient anyone who approaches too close during a power outage. "Don't walk on my property" is another one of his favorite sayings—but more about him later.

Another prepper I spoke with said that he is currently preparing for the possibility of floods, earthquakes, and tornadoes. He's also concerned about economic collapse and has several thousand ounces of silver, gold, rare coins, guns, and ammunition to help him deal with a coming financial crisis. He's done this because he believes that we have entered a time when we can no longer depend on the government to help us out. He told me that our society is unsustainable and that even if everyone does everything right, it won't be enough to save us from catastrophe. He believes that if we can't enjoy life and be happy now, then what's the point?

I've talked to many people of all sizes, wealth, and backgrounds throughout my entire lifetime. But this article is not about the few wealthy or powerful people in our society. It is about the average person like you and me who are making it our mission to prepare for whatever calamity might befall us. So I'll introduce you to a few of these extreme preppers.

I am currently preparing for the worst. I have a little more than a year's worth of food in storage in case we have to evacuate our home for any reason. A few months ago, I started preparing by storing extra water outside my house and filling the bathtub with bottled water every night. I've changed my toilet paper roll to compact rolls with less weight so that it takes less time to load up on toilet paper when necessary—and because I'm expecting fewer people at the moment, I have less waste as well.

PREPPERS' EQUIPMENT'S CHECKLIST

If you are a prepper, then you know the importance of being prepared for any disaster. Be sure to always have the necessary tools and gear on hand for survival in case of an emergency. This chapter will provide a list and brief descriptions of some basic prepper equipment that every prepper should have to ensure their safety and success in any situation.

The following are the list of items that each preparer needs to survive:

- A knife or multirole, like a Swiss army knife or Leatherman tool, is essential for making tasks easier when worse comes to worst. Having a sharp tool that will allow you to make quick work of tasks such as chopping wood, setting traps, or opening cans of food can make an enormous difference. A knife or multirole is also important for self-defense, so be sure to keep it within reach at all times.

- Hand protection is important for comfort and safety in any situation. Gloves will protect your hands from cuts, scrapes, abrasions, and the cold. Be sure to have a good pair of waterproof gloves in case you need them for the weather conditions that you are preparing for or even just for dirty tasks like gathering firewood or cleaning fish and game.

- A quality first-aid kit is essential for your health and the health of your family in case of an emergency. It should include bandages, gauze, and antibiotic ointment. And other equipment that will keep you healthy and safe. Be sure to have enough medicine on hand for any injuries that you or another member of your family might encounter.

- Medicine is important no matter what kind of situation you are preparing for. Stock up on some aspirin, ibuprofen, and antacids to have on hand for any aches or pains that you might experience. Be sure to take any medication only when absolutely necessary so that it will last longer.

- A radio that can pick up AM, FM, and shortwave bands is important for staying informed about any emergency situations or learning about local weather conditions. You could even pick up a short-wave radio to listen in on other countries in case of an emergency. Many short-wave radios can also act as a flashlight or power source.

- Flashlights are essential for any situation, from finding your way around when it is dark to finding your things during an emergency evacuation. Make sure that you have flashlights for every room in your house and that they all work properly when you need them most.

- Portable power is important for keeping electronics charged when the power goes out. Car chargers are important so that you can keep your cell phone or other portable devices charged in case of an emergency. You can also use a solar-powered charger to keep your batteries and devices charged while on the go so that you will always have access to information from radio stations or electronic devices like your GPS.

- A compass is important for navigation. The earth's magnetic field points north, so it can be used to tell which way you should head if you get lost or need to navigate around obstacles during an emergency situation.

- Headlamps are useful in inclement weather conditions and can also be used to light up rooms, paths, etc. when it is dark outside.

- Water is essential to keep you healthy and hydrated. Be sure to have plenty of clean drinking water that does not need purification at all times so that you will never run out of water during an emergency or while on the go. You may want to stock up on water bottles if you have the room because they are easy to store and carry around with you wherever you go.

- Fire is required for survival in many situations. Having emergency matches or a lighter on hand will ensure that you will always be able to start a fire when needed. You should also have at least one fire extinguisher on hand in case a fire breaks out while you are at home or while on the go. Be sure to practice how to use it properly to save lives and property whenever possible.

- Shelter is important for protection against the elements and keeping your family safe. A tent and/or sleeping bags will allow you to move from place to place easily or stay warm in inclement weather conditions if you have to evacuate your home.

- Waterproof bags are important for keeping your belongings dry, especially if you have to evacuate your home. They can also be used to keep electronics dry if you are on the go and need to protect them from water.

- A watch or wristwatch is important for helping you keep track of the time, especially during emergency situations when it may be difficult to know what time it is. It will also help you keep up with the past and understand how many days have passed since the disaster occurred or after the disaster was announced. In addition, wristwatches can also be used as tools for survival in case of an emergency.

Important Documents

- Keep a copy of important documents like copies of your prescriptions, birth certificates, and other necessary paperwork in a waterproof container on hand at all times. This will make it easier to replace these documents if they are lost or destroyed during an emergency or major disaster. I also have a copy of my will, insurance policy, and passport in my bug-out bag.

- Make sure that you keep important family documents like passports, wills, and other legal papers in waterproof containers as well. It is also a g idea to keep extra copies of these items at home so that they can be replaced if necessary. Family photos are also important because they can be used to help with identification in an emergency.

- Make sure to keep a copy of your life insurance policy, retirement plan, and other important papers in a waterproof container. In addition, keep photocopies of these documents at home as well.

- Keep a copy of your birth certificate at home with photocopies available in an emergency situation or situation where ID is necessary for survival. In addition, have extra copies of this document at home as well so that they can be replaced or used in the event the original document is destroyed during an emergency scenario.

- Keep copies of your driver's license, passport, and other important documents with your medical records and prescription information on them in a waterproof container. I keep these at all times, as well as copies of my health insurance card and prescriptions.

- Make sure to keep a copy of your life insurance policy and other important paperwork on hand at all times, especially if you use it to protect property by making sure that it is properly insured. I keep these papers in an emergency kit or easily accessible for reference if needed.

- Photocopies or digital images of important documents like prescriptions, passports, and social security cards should be kept in an easily accessible place as a reference more than anything else.

- Document the important documents that you have and make sure to keep copies of these in a waterproof container in a safe location. This way, even if you have a copy of the most important document, you can use it with confidence just in case something goes wrong with the original.

I hope this will help you in making sure that your papers are secure, easily available, and protected from damage during an emergency situation. These paper documents could matter more than any electronic documents you may have stored on a computer or electronic device like a tablet or smartphone because if they are lost or destroyed during an emergency it will be impossible for anyone to access them from their location without your paperwork.

Book 2:

Prepper Security Essential Guide During a Disaster

WHAT IS A DISASTER?

A disaster occurs when a situation worsens quickly because of events that are outside of our control. When you live everyday life, it is best to have an emergency plan with the necessities of what to do in these situations.

What are the essentials?

They are things that need to be done after a significant disaster or before one occurs. For example, a powerful earthquake will create destruction and death, and many other disasters. Basically, an emergency plan is made before these disasters occur. Still, when it comes time for them, you will need to know what to do.

WHAT IS A PREPPER?

A prepper is someone who has prepared for disasters that aren't entirely predictable, though. Some disasters can occur in your home or when you are traveling. Preppers need to know what they can do before a disaster occurs and what to do when it does.

Ultimately, we want to be prepared during the disasters that can occur and give us the ability to survive.

1. When disaster strikes.

You'll also want to secure shelter for your family if you're outside already. You can also make sure you have a plan for the unexpected.

2. Take care of nature.

You need to take care of nature and leave it alone. This means that you can't paint over rainwater tanks, dig up your well or fill in your pond. If you do that, you may not have water in the future.

3. The power grid is down, and you need to protect it.

Your power might be out for weeks or months. When the lights go out, looting usually follows. Your neighborhood may not always be as safe as it was before an emergency or disaster caused a power outage.

4. Protect your home from looters.

One of the biggest dangers during a crisis is looters. They are looking for easy targets and will attempt to take whatever they can from homes, businesses, cars, and trucks that aren't protected by security measures.

5. Staying healthy in a disaster.

When the power goes out, getting water and food can become an issue. Make sure that you have a supply of bottled water and canned foods. A camping stove is a good option, or you could get an electric campfire stove if you want the ambiance of campfires. Clean water is also a vital issue as many people don't realize that it's easy to contract diseases from dirty water. You can boil your water or get an inexpensive solar shower.

6. Protecting your family.

When disaster strikes, you need to be prepared for the possibility that some members of your family might not be with you. If this happens, it's essential to have plans in place for reuniting the family. Your first step is to get a method of communication. You can do that by getting a HAM radio license or getting a charged cell phone for each person in the household so you can call them if they aren't home when you are.

7. Research evacuation plans.

Your evacuation plan will vary depending on your location, but most people think they can quickly get out of an area if disaster strikes by driving out of the site. But what are you going to do if you can't drive? You should have information on where highways are closed, bridges or tunnels are damaged, and other issues that could impact escape routes.

8. Financial preparedness.

Financial preparedness can help you to survive unexpected disasters. Having an emergency fund set aside for disaster situations can help you handle any financial hardships during a crisis. Finances are something that people often delay dealing with until they have the time.

9. Go green.

Being green means taking care of Mother Earth in general, but it also means being prepared for natural disasters. For example, you might think that using gasoline in a generator is the best option because it runs on gas. Still, generators aren't always reliable for running 20 hours straight without interruption. An alternative would be to get 3-kilo propane or butane fueled generator and use that instead.

10. Think outside of the box.

We all think about what we would do if disaster struck every day, but how prepared are you? Think outside the box and try some things out. You can make some incredible discoveries during an emergency and enjoy something that you usually wouldn't even know about.

Check out this list for more preparedness info. You can never be too well equipped!

Your town may not be affected by any of these disasters, but some of them could likely happen to you and your family. Make sure that you're prepared to handle any disaster situation with the help of these tips. Prepare and survive!

To Protect Your Possessions During Disasters

The more precious and fragile the item, the easier it will be for it to be damaged or destroyed in a disaster. How you pack can make a difference, but some of your possessions will likely not fare well if they're buried under rubble or submerged in water for an extended period.

Aside from packing certain items in sealed containers and placing them outdoors, the following tips might help:

- Arrange essential items at eye level near exterior doors.

- Make sure you have copies of essential papers in a waterproof container.

- Arrange your items on shelves in the order that they would be used.

- Arrange heavy items on lower shelves and lighter ones on higher shelves.

- If you have several bottles of similar contents, place them together; for example, put all the bleach bottles together and all the cleaning fluid bottles together.

- Place tools, hardware, and gadgets at eye level close to exterior doors for emergencies or repairs following a disaster.

- Label boxes with permanent markers or stickers so that you can quickly identify them in storage or if they're scattered around after a disaster.

- Store weightier items on the bottommost and lighter ones on top.

- Select a place for storing all items that will be used first in an emergency. This may include canned goods, dried foods, and bottled water.

- Be sure to store a manual can opener because power outages might prevent you from using electric can openers, which are usually attached to the side of your refrigerator's door. Also, store a manual grater, paring knife, knife sharpener, and other kitchen utensils that you might need following a disaster.

- Place wet weather gear in sealed bags or plastic bins to prevent mold.

- Store items for long-term use, such as a camping stove and extra fuel in a plastic bin.

- Select larger appliances to house smaller items. For example, put the pots and pans in the oven and the coffeepots and teapots in the refrigerator.

- Decide whether you want to separate your cooking utensils from your eating utensils.

- Pack an emergency kit with a flashlight, emergency radio, extra batteries for flashlights, candles, or lamps, nonperishable foods (at least three days' worth), water (one gallon per person), toiletries (including soap, toothpaste, and toothbrushes) and medications that are essential to your survival.

- If you have a basement, store emergency supplies there.

- Keep track of where you keep your valuables when you're not home.

- Know where on your property to move valuables that might be affected by a natural disaster. For example, move valuables to the first floor if they are likely to be affected by tornados or earthquakes. Move valuables next to windows or near doors and protect them from thieves and vandals.

- Don't leave important documents at home, even if this means leaving valuable collectibles behind with neighbors or relatives who can keep them safe from water, fire, wind, and animals until the storm has passed.

- If you want to keep valuables stored in a safe, use a fireproof box and place it in your basement. The package should have four sliding locks on the front panel. Use a lock that is hard to open quickly.

- If you're worried that fire or other disasters might damage your home, consider buying an inexpensive safe. Make sure it's large enough for the items you most frequently use, and place the key where you would be unable to find it if your home burns down or if someone breaks into the house.

- Store your documents in waterproof containers such as pill bottles.

- Store essential papers, such as a deed to your home, in a fireproof box with a lock.

- Transfer your valuable documents to the digital format and burn or throw away all paper copies that do not have digital copies.

- You might want to make plans in case of a possible hurricane.

- Decide what you would do if there were a fire in your home.

- Make sure you have enough fuel for more than one day. If you had an electric generator, it might need energy as well.

- Keep cash in more than one place.

- Use caution with flammable products, such as turpentine, paint thinner and lighter fluid.

- Store flammables in a metal container.

- Make sure you have at least three days' worth of prescription medications. Consider storing more than you think you need because many pharmacies are likely to be closed following a disaster or war.

- Store medications in your refrigerator if they'll last longer that way, but make sure that it has power if there's an extended outage before cooling your prescription.

- Store batteries in a dry, cool place.

- Keep your freezer frost-free at all times.

- Or better yet, store your flammables outdoors in a metal container with a lock on it so that you can keep them secure. You can also store flammables on high ground away from trees and buildings where they will burn longer and more safely following a natural disaster or war.

Know How to Find and Secure a Hiding Spot in Case of an Emergency

You're not the only one who doesn't want to be found.

- In a life-or-death situation, it's easier for them to find you if they know where you'll be hiding.

- It could take hours for help to arrive, which is more time than anyone has at the moment after an ambush. So we need to prepare ourselves with knowledge and resources now!

- Hiding spots can save your life when all else fails. You'll never know when you'll need it, but you'll be glad you have it then.

Let's start from scratch. There are two main requirements to finding the perfect hiding spot:

1. Good enough: It needs to be a place no one would think of looking for you because no one would imagine anyone could hide there.

2. Convenient: Once you've settled on its location, it needs to be easy to get to with only the resources available at the time, which is when you'll usually be hiding in it.

You can find a good place for hiding by thinking of places where no one would look for someone to hide there, and then check if they're convenient.

Book 3:

Family Defense

HOW TO PREPARE YOUR FAMILY FOR STRENUOUS SITUATIONS

When does your family encounter a strenuous situation?

What sorts of things might be difficult for children to handle in a strenuous situation?

What can you do to prepare your family for these types of situations?

I often find myself preparing for the unknown: traveling, camping, and going to unfamiliar places. It's hard being unfamiliar with the area or context, and it's difficult when there are people nearby who are also struggling with this. I find my best approach at making these moments less scary is through preparation.

This way, if anything is missing or I forget something, I can quickly fix it before we leave. Another idea is to pack a few extra things in your child's backpack. This way, they are prepared if they lose something on their own.

Making this process more fun for your child will make them more likely to prepare for these situations. Let them know that they will be given a treat if they keep everything organized and ready to go before leaving.

We get it. It's hard to talk about what can happen in the event of a disaster. But if you don't prepare your family for these events now, who knows how they'll react when it happens?

This will cover all the crucial points you'll need to keep in mind when preparing your family for strenuous situations: what disasters are most likely in your area; how to assess and organize your home and property; what gear is essential for survival; and more. Plus, we'll give you some helpful guidelines on preparing children so that they're not frightened during an emergency.

Step 1: Assess and Prepare Your Home and Property

The first thing you need to do is assess the risk that your home faces from natural disasters and human-made hazards by completing these steps:

View an interactive map showing how likely each type of hazard is in your area.

Examine Your Home's Physical Features

Inspect your home's structure and assess whether it can withstand a load of a hurricane or other severe storm.

Look at you're building for any weak points that may make it vulnerable to fire, floods, or earthquakes.

Examine Your Property Connected to the House

Check the pipes and power lines that connect to your home.

Appraise Your Insurance Policy and Other Plans

Before you make any purchases, get an insurance policy for your house. And also, consider buying extra supplies from places such as Home Depot or Amazon based on how likely you think you'll experience those hazards. Compare your purchase to what you need before having them delivered and ready for use.

Make sure you have emergency plans for your area.

Step 2: The Most Likely Disasters in Your Area

Next, you need to recall the list of probable hazards in your area to get an idea of what disasters are most likely to happen there. For example, people in California should be more concerned about wildfires or earthquakes than flooding, while Floridians are more likely to worry about hurricanes. To help you decide what needs immediate attention and what can wait for a later time, here are some things that make each hazard more or less dangerous:

How Can You Tell If a Natural Disaster Might Affect You?

Signs of a Hurricane or Tornado

For a hurricane or tornado, follow these indicators for where they're headed next.

How Can You Prepare for a Tornado?

Find a place to shelter in a sturdy building.

Although this is not advisable, it's also possible to take shelter outside of your home if you can't reach a safe area.

How Can You Prepare for a Hurricane?

Even though a hurricane's strength depends on its category, powerful storms have similar, devastating effects.

Before a hurricane gets to you, make sure you know what to expect and where to get the latest news about it, including the following:

What Should People in the Path of a Hurricane Do?

Find a shelter as soon as possible if there is no time left to evacuate. If you can't evacuate, stay inside and prepare for the worst. Have flashlights ready, as they'll become your only source of light once the power goes out. Remember that hurricanes tend to be unpredictable, so stay alert.

The Essential Gear for Survival

Besides preparing your family and property for natural disasters, you need to have the right gear so that you can all survive until help arrives.

How can you prepare for the possibility of a major earthquake in your area?

Prepare an emergency kit that's ready for when disaster strikes.

To build your kit, include the following three things: first-aid supplies, food, and water.

You can find this checklist for what else to include in your emergency kit at ready.gov.

How can you prepare for floods?

Find a safe place to live or work based on how risky your area is and do this by checking out these indicators.

If you're in a low-lying area with no high ground nearby, try to evacuate before it's too late.

How can you prepare for wildfires?

Prepare an emergency kit that's ready for when disaster strikes. To build your kit, include the following three things: first-aid supplies, food, and water.

A friend or relative can help you by stocking the emergency kit for you, but remember that they might be sick with worry while they wait for news from you.

What Should You Do in the Event of a Nuclear Accident?

In a nuclear accident, find an area with low radiation levels or highly high-level air filters. Stay indoors until you are told to leave and always follow official instructions.

How Can You Prepare for Living in a Natural Disaster Area?

This type of preparation is made more accessible if your area's been dubbed a disaster zone.

Prepare yourself for the worst by taking the following steps:

To better evaluate what kind of equipment will be most helpful during a disaster, here's a list of things that each hazard can cause:

No matter how often you practice these safety tips, there will always be room for error. Understand that surviving is an unlikely prospect unless you seek help once it's all over. If you're lost in the woods, remember that your best chance of survival is to stay put—no straying from your route.

How Can You Prepare for an Avalanche?

The first step is to understand weather and avalanche conditions for where you're going. The third step is to prepare your equipment correctly. The fourth and final step, however, can only be learned through personal experience.

How can you prepare for extreme temperature changes?

Depending on how your body reacts with temperature changes, find a layer that works for you and pack accordingly:

Ensure your clothing layers are compatible, or they will either get in the way of one another or make it difficult to adjust as needed.

How can you prepare for heat exhaustion?

The first step in heat exhaustion is recognizing the symptoms. When it comes to heat exhaustion, four specific symptoms indicate a problem:

When heat exhaustion becomes a problem, drink water, and avoid heavy exertion. Dehydration from heat and physical activity will lead to a more severe condition known as hyperthermia. If hyperthermia keeps complicating your situation, seek medical treatment immediately.

How can you prepare for swimming in severe weather?

The best way to keep yourself safe during extreme weather events is by preparing ahead of time. When it comes to swimming in severe weather, remember that water temperature can range anywhere from around 50 degrees Fahrenheit to well over 100 degrees Fahrenheit. To avoid hypothermia, make sure you wear warm clothing that will help to protect you from unforeseen.

If hypothermia becomes a problem in the water, consider floating on your back to keep your head above water. If you're not doing too much vigorous swimming, try to remember how long it's been since you've last seen land. If it's been a while, try to stay calm and conserve energy when it matters most.

SURVIVAL SKILLS FOR CHILDREN AND THE ELDERLY

If you live in a city or ever have to leave your home with nothing but what you're wearing on your back, these survival skills could save your life. Whether it's an earthquake, a 9/11-like terrorist attack, or just the next big blizzard that's touched down in the Northeast and is headed for the rest of us soon (and we all know that will happen eventually), you'll need some skills to get through it.

People often don't take the time to learn about survival skills because it might not seem necessary—but take one look at

Hurricane Katrina in 2005 and tell me how wrong they are. To survive an emergency like this, there are things you should know beforehand.

The most important thing you can tell a child is this: Don't be afraid of being afraid. They shouldn't run away from the fear but rather realize its okay to be scared and then do something about it. It's common to be afraid when you're in an uncomfortable or unfamiliar situation. Being afraid is the reason people survive in the first place. Their fear makes them take evasive action, avoid dangerous situations, and ultimately stay alive.

All these skills are designed to save lives—especially kids. If you don't know what to teach them, pick one and start teaching them. If you run out of time, make it a family project and teach your child how to do it with your help.

With the increase in senior care, those caring for older family members must be prepared to provide the necessities to ensure their survival.

SURVIVAL SKILLS FOR THE ELDERLY

1. Prepare a simple meal from canned or boxed foods if possible, instead of buying expensive and fresh food.

2. Prepare a snack anytime you have a free moment, instead of spending money on fast food or full-service restaurants every time you get hungry.

3. If you have a single washer-dryer set, combine your laundry, then take it to the laundromat to save money.

4. Avoid higher calling rates by using a calling card.

5. Use long-distance telephone cards if you want to call out of state. These are excellent for getting in touch with family and friends and will save you money on your landline charges at home and reduce the cost of your long-distance service provider.

6. If you work and have childcare expenses, consider working at home if possible.

7. Rethink your transportation. For a short distance, use public transport or your own two legs instead of a car. If you do own a car, ride with friends if possible, to reduce the cost of gas.

8. Look into ways to earn income at home so that you will not have to go out.

9. Use community resources in your neighborhood as much as possible to keep costs down even further.

10. If you cannot afford to cut back on your expenses, live in a cheaper home or apartment rather than renting a home or apartment.

Developing Children's Emergency Preparedness

As a parent, there is perhaps nothing more stressful than discovering that a calamity has struck and that you have not been adequately prepared.

Our children are considerably more vulnerable to disasters than we are, both physically and emotionally, and it is our responsibility to ensure that they are able to survive them successfully.

All areas of disaster preparedness with children, from infancy through adolescence, are covered in detail in this guide.

Infants Disaster Preparedness

The first year of a child's life is brief, and there is already so much stress around the new arrival that you may be tempted to overlook disaster preparation for your small child.

Infants, on the other hand, are far more vulnerable to disasters than adults or even little children. Because of their weakened immune systems, even minor incidences of water pollution or an infected wound might result in death in these people.

Even when the newborn is not in immediate danger, I've witnessed parents panic out because they are worried about their child during emergencies. If you have supplies and a strategy in place, you will be more prepared to deal with a crisis.

Book 4:

Home Defense

HOME DEFENSE PLANS

Home defense is the act of defending one's dwelling from attack. Defense strategies are based on the security, mobility, and versatility of the defender's home and their weapons.

Home is the only place where a person is safe and secure. So a home should be the safest place on earth. But it's not always the case in today's world. One needs to take care of his/her home as much as possible to keep their family members safe and secure.

Home security includes physical security and psychological security also because some intruders tend to find out weaknesses in human psychology while intruding into the home of someone.

Psychological security will make you mentally prepared for any such incident so that you won't lose your cool while defending your family members, loved ones, or your home. Psychological triggers are fear, anger, adrenaline rush, which are mostly responsible for a negative outcome in any kind of self-defense situation.

Physical security includes the protection of the home, including outer walls, doors, windows, and most importantly, the house itself.

Your mobile phone can be handy in many cases while defending your home, but it is not a permanent solution because it can be easily snatched away by an intruder.

A house with large windows and openings will also make an easy target for any intruder, so you need to ensure that all openings of your house are protected with effective locks so that no one can enter into your home from outside.

Your interior walls should be well built to have sufficient strength to resist any kind of force which an intruder might use on you. So this is an important factor which should be addressed before choosing the best home defense product/plan for your home.

We should be planning our home defenses to have an efficient and quick response in case of any intrusion.

Planning a home defense doesn't need to be complicated. It doesn't require too much time and money to put plans in place. Some of the most important things that we need to consider are the following:

Security. Determine the best possible way for you and your family/loved ones to stay secure while at home, which includes security measures such as locks, alarms, bars on windows and doors, etc.

Mobility. Once you plan how your home will be protected, you should also plan on ways on how to reach your home in case of an emergency—by phone or car or even walking (even if it is only short distances).

Physical fitness. Your physical fitness should be well maintained if you have to navigate your way through your home during an emergency. You should be able to navigate in a dark room or any hole or crevice which may be present in your house.

HOME DEFENSE WEAPONS

Home defense weapons come in different shapes, sizes, and weights depending upon their usage and purpose. As already said that there is no one single best Home Defense weapon as it all depends on your need, budget, and locality. An example of commonly used home defense is:

A knife or a blade can be ideal for self-defense because it is portable and safe if used properly. The preferred way in self-defense is to be used as a last option because of its high risk. Don't ever use a knife to defend yourself against an intruder unless necessary, or you are not sure what will happen next. A large number of incidents have occurred because of knife attacks, and many people have lost their lives in such attacks. Using a blade during times of stress creates an imbalance that can cause serious injuries or even loss of life.

In some places, carrying weapons in open view can be considered illegal, so you need to carry your weapon concealed under normal daily clothes.

This is the reason there are so many countries and states have banned the carrying of lethal weapons openly after certain incidents, which caused undesirable consequences on the people and various countries.

These are some weapons which can be used for home defense:

Chemical weapons. Chemicals like chlorine gas and pepper spray can help you keep away intruders from entering into your house, but these are not preferred much nowadays because chemicals such as chlorine gas and pepper spray can also cause harm to the user or anyone who is near him/her in case of its use.

Physical weapons. We can use different types of physical weapons for self-defense.

- *Batons.* These are nonlethal weapons, which can be used for self-defense. The most common and popular version of the baton is the police nightstick.

- *Sap gloves.* They are light-weighted weapons used by police officers for self-defense and personal protection. These gloves are filled with lead shot or sand, which makes them a powerful impact weapon.

- *Baton attachments.* We can use different types of attachments to make our baton more efficient and effective in the case of home defense. Some of the most popular additions are knives, stun guns, impact grenades, etc.

- *Firearms.* They are used for self-defense in some instances when we can't use any other kind of weapon.

There are various kinds of firearms that are used for hunting, sport shooting, and self-defense.

There is no single best home defense product/plan for everyone. It all depends on your location, budget, and what situation you need to defend your home from.

For example, if you live in a high rise or a house with multiple floors, you can use an alarm system which will go off and alert the police at their nearest location who will come to check out the situation. If you live in a rural area with no emergency services nearby, you can use a stun gun as your home defense weapon and stun the intruder until the police arrive at your place.

You should also keep in mind that police usually take time to arrive at the spot of any emergency, so it is better to be prepared with your own home defense weapons and plan before an intruder enters into your property.

Home Defense Products

Before deciding on what home defense products are best suited for you, you should consider your personal needs. In other words, home defense products should be chosen according to your own personal situation. So there cannot be anyone Home Defense Product which can suit everyone's individual needs.

Home defense products usually fall into two categories:

1. *Defensive weapons.* These products are used to remove or keep away an intruder from entering into your home or otherwise harming it. They are used to incapacitate the intruder and to stop him from harming your family.

2. *Offensive weapons.* Offensive weapons are hand-held weapons which can be used in case of a defense or offense. They are usually carried by the homeowner as a means of self-defense against intruders, burglars, and other criminals.

There are various kinds of home defense products which we can use for our own protection, let us have a look at them one by one:

Home security product. Home security products are devices that help in maintaining round the clock protection around our house. There are various kinds of security products available today which will help you defend your home from intruders, first thing that you should ask yourself is whether your home needs any type of security system installed or not.

If your home is protected with a sound alarm system and you have other physical security products like bars on windows or steel doors in place, then you don't need any kind of home security system, but if your doors, windows, and walls are not protected with strong locks or have no protection at all than installing a home security system can be a good idea.

Home security systems are mostly electronic in nature, so you should make sure that it has backup batteries which can be used in case of power failure.

There are many types of home security systems available today which come with different features and advantages.

Wireless security systems. Wireless security systems are best suited for homes and or commercial buildings because they don't require any complicated wiring and the best thing is that they can be installed easily. For example, if you are looking for a wireless doorbell system for your home, then there are various kinds available in the market which you can buy depending upon your budget.

Wireless door chime. This system helps in alerting the person at the door, so he can open up and receive his visitor, it usually comes with a backup power supply in case of power failure.

Wireless home security alarm. These are the alarm systems that let you know when there is an intrusion and burglary attempt around your home. It helps in sending signals to the concerned authority so they can come and save you from any kinds of danger.

Home security systems with backup batteries. Backup batteries are used for saving data in computers or other devices, here it is used to protect your home from intruders. These types of security systems have backup batteries which can be used in case of failure in the power supply.

Wireless home security alarm systems. These are the systems that transmit your signal to the concerned authority through a wireless network so that they can come and save you from any kinds of danger.

Home security cameras. These are the surveillance cameras which let you know about things happening at home, it is very simple to use because it works with electricity, no wires required. It is also helpful in monitoring unauthorized intrusions, and they keep a record of all your activity so that you can check.

A home defense plan should include the following:

Activities, time, and locations of your family members, which will vary from one household to another.

List of signs, sounds, or attacks that can be used as an alert system. This includes sounds that could be used as an alarm system, such as ringing the doorbell during normal times, such as during the night or under heavy rain or thunderstorm when it won't disturb anyone else.

Home defense weapons, which will vary from one household to another and will also depend on the intruders. So it's better to keep a prepared list of your home defense weapons and their location so that you won't be worried about locating them in an emergency situation.

Home defense routes, which will vary from one household to another as well. It is essential for you to know where your family members are at any moment while being attacked by an intruder and what route they took during such an attack.

In case of a fire or flood or any other emergency situation involving more than one family member, there should be predefined places where these people can meet up.

These are some of the essential factors which should be taken into consideration to defend your home from intruders, these are not the only factors that you should consider, but these are some of the most important ones.

HOME SECURITY MEASURES AND ALARM SYSTEMS

Home security measures and alarm systems are the most important system that we should always look for when it comes to home defense plans for our home. Below are some of the home security measures that can be used to safeguard your house from intruders.

Security doors have a unique locking mechanism that is completely covered by the door and its door frame. This makes it difficult for someone to break into your home without using any equipment of his own.

A doorjamb system is another important Home Defense measure that you should have in your house. It works by stopping or making the door unstable when an intruder attempts to push through or open it. A doorjamb system triggers the doorbell to ring and send a signal to the people that are prearranged to receive such signals, in this way, no one is allowed to enter into your house without being noticed.

Security door locks. A good number of modern security door locks have a fingerprint feature that will help you monitor all individuals who try to enter your home or property. You can choose from various kinds of specialized locks depending upon your budget and the amount of protection that you need.

Window guards. Window guards also help in keeping intruders away from your window and also help in making it harder for burglars to break in through your windows.

Dead bolts. Deadbolts are strong and safe locks which are used indoors, windows, and other entry points of your home.

Anti-intruder alarm systems. These kinds of alarm systems have been modified and upgraded to a greater extent so they can now be used for a number of purposes such as alerting the police at the first sign of trouble, setting off an alarm when your home is under attack or intrusion by an intruder or any other unwanted person.

Home security cameras. As we have discussed earlier, these home security cameras can be used as a way to monitor your property for any intrusions. They can record all kinds of activity happening around you, so you don't miss out on anything.

Night-vision home cameras. These cameras are used to record footage at night. There are various kinds of such lenses that can be used depending upon the light conditions that you need.

Siren. A home security siren can be used in an emergency situation like a fire or flood so that you can easily get help from nearby buildings and also alert the police and other security people.

Electronic door locks. These require no keys to operate. They work on a simple touchpad or button, which makes them easy to use. Their lock is very durable and strong and will not break in case of any heavy force applied to it.

Specialized locks. There are various kinds of special locks available today which can be used for home security purposes. Some of the most popular specialty locks include-

Door chains. Door Chains are used to help you protect your home from any unwanted intruder. These chains usually come equipped with a doorknob or a locking mechanism which is hidden behind the wall; it works by creating a barrier between the door and the frame.

If you want to get the great protection for your home and family, you should buy a good alarm system. For this, you don't have to be a professional security expert. You can easily install an Alarm System in your own home, which is simple, easy to set up, and doesn't require any special knowledge or training. Also, the cost of these systems has been brought down drastically over the years so that everyone can install them without worrying about spending too much money on them.

You have to ensure that the system that you choose to use is the right one for your home and it should be able to do what it's supposed to do, if it doesn't do any of these, then its better you replace it with a better one as this will ensure maximum security.

Additional Home Security Measures

Home security kits and tools. You can also get Home Security Kits and Tools which would allow you to perform all the home defense measures in situations where you might not be able to use other items such as a gun or a knife.

Here are some examples of these tools and kits:

Police alarm. It is one of the most important measures that you can use to keep intruders at bay. You can find many different types of police alarms which are more effective if they are installed professionally.

Strobe light. They are important to give an intruder a chance to run away without getting caught by you or your family. Its bright light and sound will add to the confusion which surrounds the moment where someone is trying to break into your home, giving him a chance to escape before he gets caught.

Laser alarm. This is another important item for home security; it is very effective in preventing or repelling burglars.

Fencing. It is one of good ways to keep intruders from getting in your property, it also protects your property from the elements such as high wind and cold. You can choose from different kinds of fencing depending upon the area where you live and the amount of money you have.

You can always find these additional home security measures in the market today. They will protect you and your property from intruders at any given moment. Many of the leading companies offer a variety of home security systems for different kinds of uses, whether it is kids, seniors, or even pets. We have shared some of the popular home security systems that are very effective and easy to set up. If you want to know more about these systems, you can go online and read through all the reviews we've posted for each system so you can decide which one's best for yourself.

It's important that you take your own personal security into consideration before installing any kind of home security system or anything else for that matter, this will ensure maximum protection for you and your loved ones.

These are some of the security measures and alarm systems that will make our home much safer so that we can feel secure in our home without any fear of intruders.

PROTECTING YOUR FAMILY AND CHILDREN

Protecting your family and children from any kind of danger is of utmost importance. You should help them learn the correct way to defend themselves from any intruders or otherwise.

However, if you are in a situation that you have to leave home, you should teach them the following guidelines:

Your children must be well aware of the dangers in your neighborhood. They must know not to talk with strangers and not to accept any gifts or candy from them.

You can familiarize them with their surroundings so they would quickly know where they are going even if they are walking alone. Teach your children as early as now about safe places that they can go to, even at nighttime.

Do not keep money on the table or on your bedside table. Also, teach them to hide any valuable things in their pockets and pack them in a backpack whenever they must leave home.

In case if you have to go out of your home, teach them how to lock it securely so that it would not be possible for intruders to enter anytime soon. Also, teach them how to open the windows if they are locked.

If they must bathe in the public bath, teach them to always swim with their clothes on.

Make sure that your children would know not to talk with strangers or play in front of streets or roads. Also, make sure that they will never talk about bad things as some people might have different intentions for them.

Never allow anyone to enter your home without permission unless it is a visit from a relative. Teach them to always look for suspicious people in alleys or dark places. If you will be allowed them to play outside, teach them never to go near the fences of your home as there are many dangers lurking in there.

Give your children a list of important phone numbers such as police department and contact numbers so that they can call for help whenever they got lost while playing.

Teach your children not to approach any vehicles that are parked or unattended. Also, tell them not to talk with strangers inside vehicles because they might be bad people who could use them for their own motives.

Make sure that your children will know how to protect themselves from getting bitten by snakes, scorpions, and other poisonous animals. Also, teach them not to touch animals with their bare hands as they might have diseases, or maybe they are venomous.

In case if you have to go out of home, teach your children how to prepare food and water for them. Make sure that they should be ready whenever they left home so that they would not feel lonely while you are away.

Teach them on how to recognize what is dangerous by reading books about survival skills. Insects are here in our surroundings, and they are quite beneficial to us. Some insects play an important role in pollinating plants to have fruits and vegetables for human consumption. However, some other insects can cause severe allergic reactions with their bites or stings. You should know that there is a wide variety of insect species whose bites can cause different reactions on the skin, but some of them are responsible for many serious diseases that can result in death. To protect yourself from this kind of situation, you should take precautions against these insects, especially if you have a family or kids at home.

Other ways of protecting family and children

Protective training. You should provide your family members with protective training so that they can protect themselves in case of any kind of danger. Some of the things that you can teach your family members are-

Physical and verbal self-defense. Every member of your family should be taught how to protect himself in case he is attacked by an intruder, physical self-defense techniques like punching or kicking will help your kids be prepared for any kind of situation. Verbal self-defense techniques include-

Verbal confrontation. This is the most important technique that you can teach your family members. Always remember that their safety is more important than anything else.

Nowadays, even kids have cell phones and tablets, so it is very important to explain to them how to use these devices to alert the police in case of an emergency situation or a criminal attack. They should be taught how to call the police without drawing any attention towards themselves or their location. Also, they should be taught about calling for help while hiding in a safe place by using their cell phones.

Protective equipment. Apart from teaching your family members how to protect themselves, it is also the parent's responsibility to protect their kids from any kinds of danger by providing them with protective equipment. Protective equipment usually includes the following:

- *Safety helmet.* It is a very important piece of equipment that can help your children and other family members protect themselves from any unforeseen incident or an awkward situation.

- *Home security products.* These are various kinds of home security products that will help you keep your home safe from intruders and burglars. There are various kinds of security products available today which can be used for a number of purposes, but there are always some exceptions.

These are some of the most important factors which can help you protect your family and your children from any kinds of danger.

As a parent, it is very important to remember that you don't need to stress too much on protecting them because you need to ensure that you keep them busy with something positive so that they don't take things for granted and always remain relaxed to keep their guard up at all times.

Self-Defense for Kids

When you're young, and you hear a story about someone who has been hurt or killed by someone else, your first thoughts are usually that it will never happen to you. And when it does happen, the shock and disbelief can cause more harm than the initial encounter. That's why self-defense training can be invaluable for children who have to interact with strangers on a regular basis. Since their level of perception is still low and they tend to be impulsive, they are more likely than adults to make bad decisions on their own. The time to teach them how to defend themselves against an attacker or a violent criminal is when they're still in the early stages of development. Children nowadays are more likely to respond well to a simple self-defense session where they learn how to move, think and act faster so that if they ever have an encounter with a dangerous person, it will be over as quickly as possible.

A self-defense class for kids is not about teaching them how to hurt others. It's all about making sure that your child knows that there are steps towards protecting themselves. They might not be able to prevent an attack, but they can definitely learn how to make it end sooner than later.

In this age of cell phones and television shows and movies that focus on violence, it's important to make sure that your child knows how to protect themselves. And kids are the most vulnerable to copycat behavior as they're quick to learn from what they see around them. Their ability to learn is very high compared to adults because their brain has not yet completely developed and they are able to store a lot of information before developing the capacity for rational thinking and complicated reasoning.

It's best if you teach them self-defense before they even start school. The earliest sign of trouble is when a child feels threatened by another child or sees something that makes him feel unsafe in public or at home. But even if your child never faces an actual physical attack, it's important to encourage them to learn self-defense so they can be prepared in case they ever do have an encounter with a violent criminal.

Building self-esteem is one of the most essential things you can do as a parent because not only does it help your child feel better about themselves in the long run, but it also helps them to become more successful and able to defend themselves. It will also make them more confident about their actions and decisions, which will probably save them from the mistakes that so many other people end up making after experiencing a violent crime or two.

Preparedness Is the Key

Preparedness is the key; no one is safe from any kind of danger and or any unforeseen incident. So it is very important that you should remain prepared for all kinds of situations so you can easily deal with them when they arise. You should help your family members remain prepared as well so that they can react properly and safely in case of any kind of danger or emergency situation.

Always remind yourself to keep your eyes open for any signs of trouble that could threaten your family and or property, if you ever spot something unusual, then be sure to take the right steps to make things normal again. If you are not aware of anything, then you can always involve the proper authorities so that they can take care of things for you.

The above-mentioned home defense plans are meant to help our homes stay secure, so we don't feel unsafe in them, but keeping all these procedures in place isn't enough. We must also practice this at all times. You should always remain alert even in your daily routine; there is no reason you should remain unaware of what is happening around you and around other people. Basically, you should always be prepared to react properly in case of any kind of danger.

Book 5:

Energy Defense

WATER

In favorable circumstances, a properly hydrated individual will survive little more than three days without water. Far less when facing intense temperatures and lack of shelter. Our bodies are comprised primarily of water that is subject to continual loss, therefore, it must be frequently replenished. On average, we lose one to three liters a day. Sweat, breathing, digestion and bodily functions all contribute to this loss. When in a survival situation, finding water, consumption of water, and water loss must always be accounted for. Many times, it will take precedence over the other necessities on our list. This need is persistent and will require attention on a daily basis.

Retention

Our first defense is to protect the reserves that we already have. Good decisions and simple actions can make a veritable difference. If heat and pounding sun are a factor, this is the time to take shelter. Find a cool place that is shaded. Do not overexert yourself and cause excess sweating. Never lie directly on the hot ground. Clearing away the soil on the surface will reveal a cooler area below. Breathe through the nose at a slow and even pace. Talking and respiration from the mouth will work against you.

Eating should be kept to a minimum. Digestion will draw fluids from the body and cause the need for excretion which will take even more. Foods containing high protein and fats are the worst culprits. Processing alcohol demands fluids from the vital organs and will always because more harm than good. Energy drinks and soda are also not a recommended choice for rehydration. Caffeine is a diuretic and the high concentration of sugars in these beverages pulls water through the kidneys that cannot be reabsorbed. Smoking dehydrates you as well, so save cigarettes as tinder for fire-building.

When water quantities are sparse, sip from what you have and consume it over time. To guzzle large amounts will dilute the bloodstream and it will be lost through the kidneys. When you are dehydrated, too much water in the stomach can also cause nausea and vomiting which is a severe waste of fluids. Stay away from drinking any unpurified water as well. Bacteria can produce sickness that will lead to diarrhea and vomiting. This combination will quickly put you in a dire situation.

Water Collection

Fortunately, water is one of the most abundant resources on the planet. Because we are so dependent on it, most of the population lives in proximity to water. Finding a continuous source is the best scenario and you always want to look for more water before you run out. Incidentally, you may find yourself in some of those places where water is scarce. When this is the case, you might need to rely on numerous methods of procurement. There are various bits of knowledge which can improve your chances.

Initially, the properties of water will give us some clues as to where it can be found. We know that it runs downhill and collects in low-lying areas. It is also subject to evaporation, so we must look in places that are protected from the sun's rays. Seek out valley bottoms or the base of hills and ravines. It is known that water is held in the earth. Dig in the lowest points of a dry pond or the outside bends of drained riverbeds.

After evaporation, it is returned in the form of rainfall. Be ready to capture it with a poncho or tarp when it does. Large plant leaves can also be used to catch or funnel rain into containers. Even laying out clothing to soak up rain can provide ample quantities. Rainwater will also become trapped in the depressions of stones or rocky terrain. If gathered from a clean surface, rainwater will not need to be purified.

The needs of plants reflect our own, so any places with gathered vegetation will be a good indicator. In areas that water is slight, these patches of green will contrast the surroundings and should be easy to pick out. Some plants that live in dry climates will store plentiful reserves of water inside. In Africa and Australia, the baobab tree holds vast amounts of water and has been used for thousands of years. Search the tree, and you will likely find a tapping hole that has been used by natives for generations. This tree is endangered, and the thick bark should not be tapped unless it is a complete emergency.

A succulent dollar bush can be pressed to get bitter juices. It is recognizable by the flat round leaves. You can also obtain fluids by cutting off the top of a barrel cactus and squeezing the fleshy insides. This fluid will have a milky color which, as a rule, you should avoid, but the barrel cactus is an exception. The prickly pear cactus also holds a lot of moisture in the reddish yellow fruit and the flat ears of the plant itself. Cut away the spines of the cactus before handling it.

Soaking up the dew that collects on non-poisonous plants is another superb way to gather water. In the morning, use a piece of cloth to absorb dew from green plants and wring it out into your mouth or a container. Surprisingly, these small drops can add up to a decent amount in a short time. Sometimes the crevice between two trees that separate near the trunk will collect water that can be taken to boil.

In the springtime, maple and birch trees can be tapped for fluids. Cut a V shaped gash into the trunk with your knife. Cut past the bark and slightly into the inner tree. When the sap begins to run out, insert a small stick to direct the fluid into your container. Warm sunny days after a cold night will be the best time to tap a tree.

Vines with rough bark are generally a good source as well. Follow the vine to the highest place that you can reach and cut a notch with your knife. Now, go to the bottom and cut the vine off where it comes out of the ground. The notch on top will let air into the vine and increase the flow of liquid from the bottom. Collect what drips out, unless it is sticky, has a milky appearance, or is bitter tasting. The sap or juices taken from plants should not be kept more than twenty-four hours or it will begin to ferment and spoil.

In the tropics, many plants will naturally catch water in their broad leaves or it will be held in reservoirs at the center of bromeliads. Banana and plantain trees can be cut down at the base of the trunk and when a hollow is cut out of the trunk, the roots will fill fresh water into the hole. Discard the first three fillings—as it will be too bitter—but after that, it will be potable. Cover the trunk to keep the bugs out and it will last up to four days.

The milk from unripe green coconuts is good. Mature coconuts contain an oil that will act as a laxative and this should only be consumed in limited amounts. They can be a precious food source. Get coconuts down with a forked branch, climbing or dislodging them by throwing other coconuts.

Bamboo can provide for you as well. Bend over a couple of green stalks and stake them to the ground. Cut off the tops and water will drip from them during the night. The hollow trunks of older bamboo will catch water if it has a crack in it, but it will need to be purified. Palms, such as the buri, coconut, sugar, and nipa will drip fluid when one of their lower fronds is pulled down and the inner tree is exposed. They will also bear liquid if the tip of a flower stalk is cut off.

The juices can be taken from many kinds of fleshy plants. A lot of different roots will also give water when the bark is stripped off, and they are pressed or fluids are sucked out. It is critical that these plants are positively identified and known to be free of harmful toxins. The best way to remove the water from many living plants is to create a solar still.

You will need a plastic bag or a plastic sheet that can be folded over and sealed. A plastic tarp, tent material, or poncho can work for this process. It is best to have clear plastic so that the sunlight can penetrate the bag and draw more water from the plants. Fill your bag about half-way full of vegetation. Tear apart broad leaves and make sure that there will be nothing to puncture the plastic. A rock inside the bag will keep it from blowing away. Fill the bag with air and seal it tightly.

Now, place the bag into direct sunlight. Condensation will form on the plastic and run to the bottom of the bag. Do not let it leak from tiny holes that may be in the bottom. Place the hole over a container if this is a problem. Replenish the plant material as needed. This can also be done by tying the bag directly onto a leafy branch so that the water collects in the corner of the bag.

Animals and insects can point us in the right direction when we watch for the signs. Herbivores are generally not far from a source of water, especially larger grazing animals that habitually drink in the morning and evening. Look for droppings and find game trails. Heavily trodden paths where other trails converge will regularly lead to water if followed downhill. Carnivores are not good indicators.

Grain-eating birds tend to stay near water and will drink in the mornings and evenings. Watch to see how they fly. If heading to water, their flight will be low and direct. After drinking, birds will move from place to place and stop frequently to rest. During migration, many water birds will head for bodies of water or marsh areas in the evening when they stop to rest for the night. In the morning they can be seen and heard leaving these places.

Observing the patterns of certain insects can also be exceptionally reliable. Bees make their hives close to a dependable source and do not often fly more than a few kilometers from water. Ant colonies rely on water and following a steady column of ants can reveal a hidden cache. It may be a small crevice or notch in a tree that might require a strip of cloth to soak it up. This can be a huge windfall in arid climates. Normally, you will not find a fly more than a hundred meters from water, so they will also indicate that you are close.

Our bodies require elevated levels of water in cold climates. Paradoxically, our thirst and desire to drink is driven down in these places, so it is important to maintain hydration. Gathered snow and ice should be boiled. Cold temperatures will not kill bacteria. Melting ice is preferred over snow. It will yield more than double the amount of water and require only half of the heat to do so.

If you are melting snow in a metal container over direct heat, it is best to add the snow slowly until there is a decent base of water in the container. Otherwise, you will scald the bottom of your container. Clean, freshly fallen snow will not need to be boiled but it is best to melt it first. Eating snow requires extra energy to process and cools the body. Both things will deplete valuable calorie reserves.

Coastal ice will become desalinated after about a year and will begin to have a bluish color. After two or more years this ice will be almost completely free of salt. Grey or opaque sea ice will contain too much salt to safely drink. Ice taken from glaciers, rivers, and lakes has been used by natives of the Polar Regions for thousands of years. These sources are still relied upon by the indigenous people of the frigid arctic regions.

When you are stranded at sea, there are not a lot of options for fresh water. Seawater should never be consumed without desalinating. To do so will speed up dehydration. If this is continued over time, the body will progressively weaken from poisoning. The end result will be madness and death.

Capturing rain at sea should always be taken advantage of. Heavy dew is common and can be soaked up or gathered from the air with a sail that has some slack in the bottom to catch the dew when it runs down. If you have a way to boil the salt water, the steam can be collected on the underside of an angled plastic sheet so that the condensed water runs to a collection point.

With the right materials, it is also possible to make a solar still at sea. A large and small container can be used with a plastic covering. Put some seawater in the large container and place the small container in the center of the larger one. The small container will be empty so make sure that it does not float or move from the center. Cover the large container with the plastic and seal it by tying the edges. Put something weighted in the center so that the condensed water will run down the inside and drip into the small container.

In many cases, fish will be one of the best sources when it comes to replenishing fluids at sea. Fish contain high levels of water in their bodies. As a rule, ordinary-looking fish with normal scales and fins will be safe for consumption. It is recommended that you pass on anything that has an irregular appearance—especially when in warm waters.

The juices can be obtained by cutting the fish into pieces and chewing out the liquids. If eating is not an immediate requirement, spit out the solids and use them to catch more fish. You can also put the pieces of fish into cloth and wring out the liquids into a container. Many larger fish will also have a water reservoir near their backbone that can be tapped and drained.

Decontamination

Finding a source of water is not a huge complication most of the time. Often, the problem will be locating water that is ready to drink. Dew, water from plants, freshly fallen snow or rain, and that taken from fish or the eyes of animals, are the few places that you can get water which will not need to be made potable. There is no guarantee, though. There are many rumors surrounding drinkable water, but the bottom line is, that there is no dependable way to determine the safety of water outside of a laboratory. To drink contaminated water in a survival situation will most likely lead to sickness that, without immediate rescue and medical attention, could edge you dangerously close to death.

It is easy to believe that a source of water should be safe to drink from. This lie will become more acceptable as your thirst grows and you become desperate. That crystal-clear mountain brook might contain the carcass of an animal rotting upstream. The most pristine lakes and rivers are still full of microscopic protozoa, bacteria, and viruses. Waterborne diseases account for approximately three and a half million deaths every year. Be smart, be safe, and survive. When it comes to life and death, look at every source of water as contaminated.

Even those listed above can pose some risk if they come in contact with the wrong surface. On a microscopic level, it only takes one drop. If you don't believe my warning, take some time to do a bit of research on a few topics: cholera, cyclosporiasis, dysentery, hemorrhagic fever, typhoid, Guinea worm disease, cryptosporidium, gastroenteritis, giardiasis, hepatitis E. This list is surely not complete, but it will hopefully be enough to knock out any doubt that you might have.

Before taking water from a source, it is best to do a visual inspection. Look for oil on the surface. Be sure that there are no dead animals nearby. When there is no green vegetation, or you see bones present, it is a safe bet that it is poisonous or dangerously contaminated.

Aside from boiling, few of the water treatment methods will be fully effective at removing all pathogens. This will require a metal container to boil in and the ability to make fire. If you came prepared with a container, filter and the means to build a fire, then you are in good shape. There is varied advice on the boil time, but to hold a rolling boil for ten minutes will provide complete reassurance in any circumstance.

There could be times that you need to improvise a container to boil in. This could be made from wood or something that cannot be moved over a fire. Use the primitive method of boiling with fire-heated stones placed into the container of water.

Boiling does not get rid of any chemical contaminants that may be present but in most wilderness locations this should not be a critical issue. It will not remove particulate either, so you are still dealing with dirty water. The dirt will not hurt you, but it is understandably not favorable. When possible, it is recommended that the water is filtered before boiling.

Filtering

The filtering process can range through a spectrum that begins with primitive simplicity and ends with the inclusion of modern science. In its most simple form, this will remove large pieces of sediment and plant or animal matter. The most technologically advanced filter is able to clear out particulate, protozoa, bacteria, and most viruses. Even the best portable filters will not take away chemicals and heavy metals, though.

To simply separate larger debris it is possible to slowly pour water through layers of grass and a piece of cloth. By itself, a handkerchief can catch quite a bit of sediment. After this, let the water sit for about an hour. Much of the fine silt will settle to the bottom. Carefully take the top three-fourths of the water without stirring up the sediment. Depending on the source of the water, it could very well have a brownish color due to tannins that are left from decayed plants. Do not worry about the color.

A better filter can be made with a plastic bottle, sock, shirt sleeve, or separate layers of cloth that are tied to a tripod framework. I will explain how to make one with the bottle because it will better ensure that the water is forced through the filtering agents and does not just bypass them by soaking through the fabric. If you do not have a bottle, use the illustrations below and the process will be the same. The second choice would be the series of cloth catch-basins and a tripod.

A larger plastic bottle or jug will give you the ability to process more water. If it has a cap, poke a few holes in it with your knife. Now, cut the very bottom of the bottle off. If the mouth is large and you do not have a cap it might first need a couple of sticks set crossways to block it up somewhat. On top of that, you can place a bed of moss, grass, or cloth. Over the bed, you will place a layer of partially crushed black coals from a previous fire. The coals can be covered with a layer of dry sand.

Now, add some larger pieces of coal. It should be topped off with a good layer of small pebbles or the coal will want to float when you add water. With a couple of holes in the top edge and some cordage, you will be able to suspend it above a container to catch the end product. Slowly pour water in the top and continue to refill the filter as it cycles through.

It is also possible to use something called a ground filter. This can be exceptionally useful in swamps, marshlands, or near a saltwater coast. Find a spot that is above the water line and dig a hole that is about elbow deep and just as wide. Water will begin to seep through the ground. Let it fill and then take from the top where it is clearer. Near the coast, you must be above the high tide line. Freshwater is lighter and should settle above the saltwater line. Stop digging as soon as you see water seep in because a deeper hole will give water with a higher salt content.

Something similar to this is a below ground still. A hole should be dug in a sunlit area and should not go all the way down to the water line. At the bottom, you will place a container in the center where the condensed water will drip. Like the solar still, you can also situate vegetation around the container to add extra moisture. If you can salvage some plastic tubing from somewhere, this can be added to the still so that you do not need to take everything apart when the container fills up.

Cover the hole with plastic so that it hangs down in the middle like a funnel. The edges will need to be covered with dirt or rocks so that the plastic does not fall inward. A stone in the center will direct the condensed water into the container. Dirty or stagnant water can be poured onto the ground near the sides of the hole. This water will be filtered as it seeps through the ground and adds moisture to the still. When using vegetation, it must be changed every few days or it will begin to rot.

When it comes to portable filters, there is a multitude of options and the technology is changing every day. Some use ultraviolet light, adsorptive filters use a special magnet to attract contaminants. The various types of micro-filters trap material as the water passes through. All of them have positive and negative attributes. This market is constantly seeing changes and improvements.

My best advice is to do the research and read reviews before purchasing. Figure out what type of filter will best suit your needs, as there are many choices. Look at the capacity of water it will filter. Make sure that you know how it works and what specific contaminants it will remove. Depending on your needs, it could be prudent to have three different filters for separate locations. Think about your day pack, car, and home.

Many portable filters will not remove viruses, and depending on which part of the world you are in this could be a major factor. I prefer to use a filter in conjunction with boiling to be on the safe side. When dealing with dirty water, it is good to prefilter with primitive means or let the water settle.

Particulate will clog or slow down most filters. Using cleaner water will expand the lifetime of most portable filters and improve their efficiency. Note that when the water inside certain types of micro filters becomes frozen it can destroy the capability of the filter's integrity.

Chemical Decontamination

There are a number of different chemical agents that are commonly used to make water potable for drinking. Many of them have been in use for a long time and others are new to the market. Usually, these are good at killing viruses but cannot always be relied upon to destroy protozoa. Again, this is an area where you will need to check the facts if you believe that this might be a good option for you.

One good thing about most of these is the fact that they are compact and easy to put into a small survival kit. Keep in mind that when using chemical decontaminants, the dosage must align with certain proportions. Not enough additive could prevent it from working and too much could make you sick. Often these agents do not work instantaneously and will give an unpleasant flavor to the water. Make sure to fully read instructions before use. In the right place, these can be a good thing to have.

Salt

A minute intake of salt on a daily basis coincides with the importance of water. The body requires about 10 mg of salt to regulate fluids. It is consistently lost through sweat and urination, therefore must be replaced. In hot weather, our reserves are depleted even faster. When the body is running low on salt, you will have a hard time quenching thirst. It will progress to weakness and lack of energy.

Next, there will be muscle cramps, dizziness, and nausea. The body will feel very hot and dry. Watch for these signs in yourself and other survivors. Upon recognition, dissolve a pinch of salt into one liter of water. Fluids, salt, and rest will be the fastest means of treatment.

It is not a bad idea to have some salt tablets or a small bottle of coarse salt with your survival gear. Most modern foods and survival rations have plenty of salt added to them for flavor and natural preservative. Wilderness food that you gather, on the other hand, will be largely deficient. Tribes across the globe have used animal blood as a solution to this problem for ages and still do today. Animal blood is rich in valuable minerals and a viable source of salt.

Small amounts of seawater can be added to your fresh water in a ratio of about one to eight parts. Seawater can also be evaporated, and the crystals gathered afterward. Salt is also obtainable from the roots of hickory trees and nipa palm. Boil the roots until all the water evaporates and then collect the black salt crystal deposits.

Dirt Time

Now that we understand the importance of boiling, it is imperative that you obtain a reliable container for this process. Tackling water challenges without it will be exceedingly difficult. As a companion to that, investigate different filter options and find something that is right for you. Once those items are checked off the list, it will be time for some practice.

Think about your climate zone and the places that you travel to. What are the bits of knowledge that are most pertinent when it comes to locating water? If you spend time at sea, apply what you have learned and expound upon it. If you live in an arid environment, train yourself to find those hidden water sources.

Everyone would do well to seek more information about the plants in your area that can provide for you. Also, take the time to closely observe the indicative patterns of animals and insects. When times get tough, these are huge windfalls and should never be discounted.

Now that you have learned more about meeting survival needs in your area, start testing the techniques described in this chapter. Construct each of the different types of still. Try to start from scratch and make a functional filter. Make the fire to get the coal. Find a bottle in the wilderness or use a sock. Gather the different materials for the layers that make up the filter.

Identify and extract fluids from the correct plants. On paper, the pictures and descriptions are not a big deal, but you will find that by working through these different procedures, it will pose certain complications. These complications will refine your skill. You will learn tricks to improve your technique, find out how much can be garnered from different plants and determine the amount of water that can come from an efficient still.

Water needs will often be the biggest obstacle that you need to overcome. To master these things is a huge accomplishment and one of utmost importance. Take great pride in your ability to prevail over this stage in the survival process.

POWER

Bug-Out

Bug-out power requirements are the easiest to prepare for as they have limited power requirements. They are:

1) Cellphones, walkie-talkies, CB mobile radios

2) Lighting

3) Radios, emergency, weather, AM/FM

4) Tablets, small laptops

The power requirements for these devices are fairly low and can be satisfied by solar and hand-crank generators. Combination solar panels/battery packs are very popular for emergency power sources. Here are some ideas:

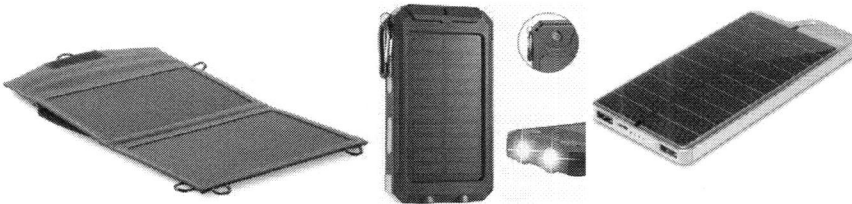

These solutions work great as long as there is sunlight. What if it is overcast or it is at night time? There are two other choices.

Wind:

Combo wind/solar units

And Hand Power:

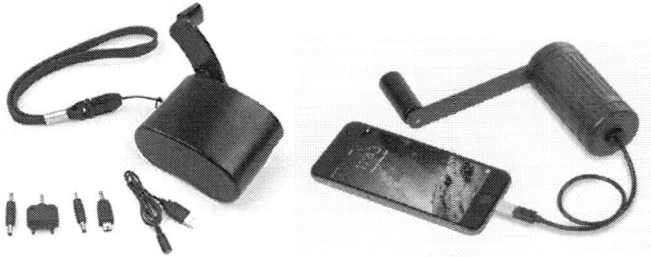

Hand crank charger/radio units

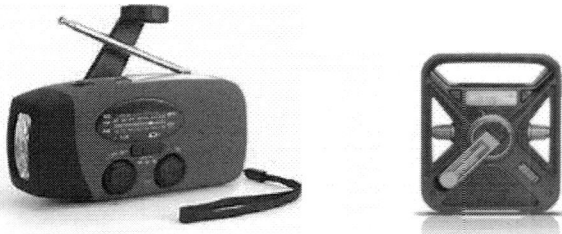

Back-up power for bug-out events is critical as many services such as communications and the internet may still be operational. You may want to include more than one solution in your bug-out bag.

Emergency Events

Power requirements for the emergency events model encompasses those for the bug-out model but because of the possible extended event duration some additional power sources may need to be added. This assumes that you have more cargo carrying capacity than the bug-out model. The following are some choices:

Gas Power Generators

Small, quiet generators are readily available for good prices. These are useful for intermittently powering higher power appliances or charging battery banks when solar or wind is minimal. Naturally a good supply of fuel is required.

Larger Solar Panels

Beyond the small portable style solar panels, larger panels providing enough power to charge a battery bank and provide adequate power you're the electrical devices are needed.

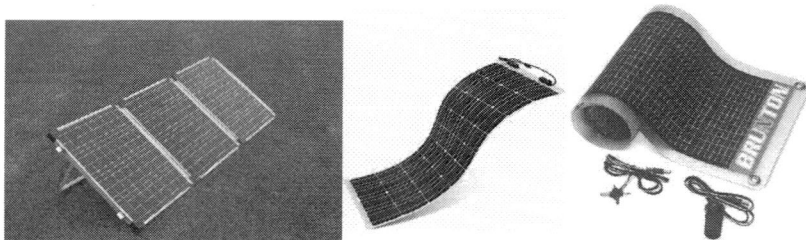

Battery Bank

Use larger batteries for making a bank that can retain a charge from your gas generator, solar and wind generation. While lead-acid batteries will work, they are heavy – NiCad or lithium is best. More battery bank information is in the next model.

Some examples of these are:

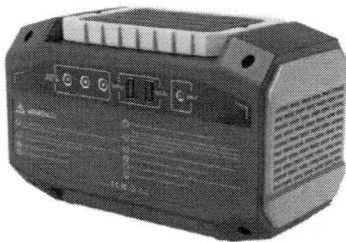

Battery banks are heavier and are definitely not for backpacking travel. But they do fit well in most vehicles, and should be already in your car or truck as a given.

Prepper Hacks

The following are some beneficial 'hacks' for power.

- Have old car alternators around? They make workable power generators – wind, water, pedal powered.

- Lighting for important items can be done without power. Just paint them with glow-in-the-dark resin paint.

- Want bright lights for temporary emergency needs? Hook one end of a 2-6' fluorescent bulb to an antenna being fed by a CB radio. The RF energy will light the bulb.

- Use a bicycle friction generator to charge USB devices. You just connect the right USB power wires to the output through a simple regulator.

- If you are using lead-acid batteries and they become non-functional, open the cases and retrieve the lead plates. Use protective gear (masks and rubber gloves, etc.) as lead can be unhealthy. This lead can be used for ammo, air gun pellets, fish sinkers, and other items.

Book 6:

Health Defense

MEDICAL AND HEALTH

Bug-Out

Because of the length of a bug out model event, extensive medical supplies and equipment will need to cover mostly minor trauma cases, and be small and light. Organic illness that occurs over a period of time will be covered in the succeeding models. The most possible medical needs during a bug-out model (and even an emergency event) are; cuts, blisters, fevers, colds, headaches, eye irritation, rashes such as poison ivy, etc., bruises, stomach upsets, and stress. Since nothing more serious than these are probable, your medical kit should support at least these. If there is room, then supplies for splints and wrappings for sprains or minor breaks can be included. Also, antidepressants, pain relief ointments and anti-fungal lotions could be included. There are many small medical kits that have supplies to cover most of these cases. Start with the basic medical kit and supplement it with additional items if you feel the need. Here are some small medical kits:

Emergency Events

Since emergency events may last longer than a typical bug-out event, additional health considerations need to be addressed. The most important is supplementing the basic emergency rations with important nutrients to maintain optimum health. Emergency rations like MREs and home-brewed rations main purpose is to keep you alive and provide your body with fuel. Even though many of these have some nutrients included, it may not be enough Thus, a good supply of vitamin and mineral supplements should be included.

In addition to the basic medical kit in your bug-out bag, an emergency event might require additional items from the medicine cabinet. More pain killers - internal and topical, more field dressing supplies, and medicines for normal sicknesses, alcohol, hydrogen peroxide, and ointments. Check into military field medical kits that have more extended trauma equipment and supplies.

The "Big One"

Outside of a military field hospital, what medical facilities can be saved in this model is quite varied. And, if you are sheltering with other preppers in a cooperative manner, having more extensive medical facilities individually may not be needed –

you may have a communal medical clinic. But it is obvious that you will no longer have ERs, ICUs, exotic diagnostic systems and trained specialists like is currently found in large metropolitan hospitals. If it is possible beforehand, a more extended collection of medical supplies and equipment, even prescription type drugs should be procured. Even if there is no trained medical specialist in your immediate evacuation group, there may be future contacts with medical specialists that will be bartering their services. Medical equipment and supplies are good **counter-barter assets** to have.

As in all of these models, your critical medical documentation including drug prescriptions should be with you. See protective document holders in the 'Documents' category.

Health Maintenance

Along with treating any sickness or injury, keeping yourself and family members healthy is critical as the disaster time becomes more extended, or whether it is at a SHTF stage. If you eventually settle in a place where gardens can be grown, then this will take care of most needs. Also learn about what wild foods have specific nutrients and supplement what you may have with these. Until that time you will only have your emergency rations and supplements to ensure that you do not become nutritionally deficient.

Medical Drugs

Along with maintaining your health through optimum nutrition, there will be certain times when a drug will be needed. This is especially true if you have a medical condition that requires regular medications. Since in a SHTF model, the manufacture and distribution of pharmaceutical drugs will be vastly reduced or eliminated, now would be a good time to deeply research natural alternatives to those drugs, or even more plentiful generic ones. Of course, stocking up on your special drugs is difficult to do legally, but you can fudge what you take and squirrel away a small excess. This works if the drugs have long shelf life. You should stockpile a good supply of OTC drugs that are effective, like; Neosporin, Pepto-Bismol, eye drops, calamine lotion, cough syrup and drops, hydrocortisone, Lysterine, and castor oil.

Outside of weight loss and anti-depressants, the most common drugs are pain killers (especially aspirin), and antibiotics. While the pain killers are beneficial, the antibiotics are especially valuable as they can keep you from dying. As a source for antibiotics, research animal medicines - birds, equine, and fish. Check the links in the table for some sources.

Prepper Hacks

The following are some beneficial 'hacks' for medical and health.

- All-around common foods and ingredients that are almost 'magic' in what they can do; honey, apple cider vinegar, baking soda, Epsom salts, and hydrogen peroxide.

- Quick drying Super Glue can quickly close a cut. Pull the skin edges together and apply the glue.

- Research Fish antibiotics as a substitute for hard-to-get human ones. They are not prescription controlled and you can build up a stock. See the links in the table.

- Stock a number of glass thermometers.

Book 7:

Disaster Preparation

Disaster preparation is, first and foremost, about awareness. Planning is a critical step in the process, but you also need to be prepared for the worst.

What are your specific needs? Where are vulnerable areas in your home or business? What would happen if there was no power for three days? How much water do you need to have on hand in case of emergency?

It's time to be proactive and think ahead. This will walk you through some simple steps that could make an all-too-real catastrophe less devastating.

DO YOU HAVE A PLAN?

Making a plan will help you think realistically about handling a crisis and reducing the chance that panic will set in.

Create a Family Emergency Plan. Everyone needs to know their specific roles, including where they need to go, who they are going with, how they will get there, phone numbers for everyone involved, and how much food/water/clothing they should take. It's also essential for kids to know not to open the door for anyone until an adult says it is okay.

Understand your surroundings. Consider sandbagging as a way to mitigate flooding.

Have an emergency kit ready? You should have supplies ready to go at all times. Think about what items you are most likely to need in the event of an emergency. The following are suggested things to keep in the kit:

Water—at minimum one gallon per person, each day for at least three days. Plan to use bottled water if you can't boil it for any reason.

Nonperishable food, including canned food, dried food, or ready-to-eat packets. Also include snack foods and crackers that can be eaten without heating, such as beef jerky or protein bars.

Clothing and personal items—extra shoes, warm clothes for everyone in your family (wool hats and gloves), additional medication, or essential documents.

Flashlights and batteries.

A first-aid Kit.

Any special needs items, such as a portable toilet or a device to help those with disabilities.

HOW TO PREPARE FOR DISASTERS IN YOUR AREA

Since disasters can happen anywhere at any time, you want to be prepared no matter what your situation is.

So what can you do? Well, we've put together all about how to prepare for disasters—whether they strike your friends or family in an area different from yours or whether it's the disaster that affects you.

Whether your area is hard-hit by a natural disaster, such as floods or earthquakes, or it's a more common threat like a hurricane or tornado, you can prepare for disasters by following these tips:

1. Turn on the news. It's probably not news that these disasters happen all over the world.

You can also read newspapers or watch TV news bulletins to learn more about any disasters that have been reported.

2. Think about your situation. There are different kinds of natural and human-made disasters that can happen to you and your family:

3. Study the news reports. After you get a general idea of what happened, try to find out as much detail as possible about the destruction an area has suffered.

4. Determine how you'd like to help. Do you feel like you should go and help neighbors in an area hit by a natural disaster? Maybe you have more of a reason—as an engineer, for example, or as a volunteer firefighter?

5. Talk to your family. Tell them that there is a possibility of a physical disaster occurring, and encourage them to prepare for it, such as stocking up on water and other supplies.

6. Look at the area map. If a flood or tornado has damaged your area—say, this is the map of where you live—then look for an evacuation route that will get your family to safety quickly.

7. Prepare for safety first. Find food and drinking water, keeping warm, and more after your secure safety. All these helps you survive in a disaster.

8. Have a plan for your family. Take care of your family in a disaster situation is just as important as how to help others. How can you protect your children? Can you keep them safe from wild animals? Are there any dangerous plants on your property?

9. Assess your home. Because you already know some of the places that may be affected by a natural disaster, look at the area

map and find any areas that would have been hit hard by flooding or tornadoes.

10. Stock up on water. Usually, the most important thing to do is to eat and drink as much as possible. Water is essential because it'll keep your body hydrated—and it's also a good source of liquid if you have to do a lot of walking, like in an evacuation scenario.

11. Find out which food items are best to have on hand. High-energy food items like protein bars and trail mix can help get your energy running again after a long period of sleep or physical activity.

12. Be ready for cold weather. In a disaster, you won't want to be wearing all your warm clothes, and you'll probably want to wait for temperatures to rise. You'll have to have at least a layer of warm clothing on.

13. Take supplies with you if you need to leave your area. If disaster strikes, get your family together and collect as many supplies as possible first before driving out of place into safety.

14. Prepare for medical problems. In a natural disaster that takes out power grids or water systems, people may become sick because of a lack of medical care in the affected area. Try to make sure that you have adequate medical supplies on hand.

15. Think about what you're going to do when disaster strikes. An emergency plan that tells your family where to go in case of a natural disaster.

16. Consider moving away from an area at risk for earthquakes or floods. If it's possible, it's also intelligent to relocate yourself and your family away from an area that has been known to be damaged by flooding or earthquakes in the past.

17. Look at your car. If you have to evacuate, you'll need transportation to get away. If the flood or tornado damaged your vehicle, consider getting a new car and keeping all of your supplies in that vehicle.

18. Be prepared for home invasions. Determine how you would like to protect your family from home invasions in case of a disaster, and look into getting home security systems installed at different locations around your house.

19. Plan for after the disaster. Once the crisis is over, it's essential to relocate yourself or your family to another safer area.

PLANNING, PREPARATION, AND PREVENTION

Prepare for the worst with these disaster prevention tips!

It's not always easy to predict natural disasters, but thankfully there are ways to minimize your risk of them happening. From preparing an emergency kit to making sure you know how your home is insured, these disaster prevention tips will ensure you're ready in the event of a disaster.

It's essential to be prepared for a disaster in your area. Disasters are unpredictable and can strike at any time. But being prepared can help you avoid or minimize the effects of a disaster.

Find out if there is an evacuation route from where you live, work, or study that doesn't pass under trees or over hills during heavy storms.

Don't forget to plan for safety and comfort in the absence of electricity.

Make a family emergency evacuation plan.

Know where your neighbors live, work, or study so you can help them if they are in need.

Fill up your gas tank before a significant storm so you won't be left with a severe shortage of fuel afterward.

If you work in or near a school, learn what to do if there is a threat of an active shooter.

Check for gas leaks before a storm is about to hit or during the shower at your home, business, or place of worship if that's where you're providing emergency services. This will prevent fires from destroying homes and businesses.

Avoid overloading extension cords and appliances with heavy loads like clothes and furniture; they can cause fires if they get caught in a nearby wall heater, portable heater, or another device.

Put away anything that can burn at least six feet above the floor: fireplaces and logs, flower pots, stoves, grills, outdoor heaters, and other appliances.

Increase the distance from tall buildings. If you live in a high-rise building, stay in your building if it is safe to do so. Take the stairs unless an alternate object will prevent you from falling, such as a railing.

Make sure your home has fire extinguishers, especially ones that can be used indoors.

Has an emergency kit packed and ready for use at all times? Your equipment should have a battery-powered or hand-crank radio, extra flashlights and batteries, a first-aid kit, food, water, and additional medication.

BATTERIES, EMERGENCY CANDLES, AND LIGHTERS

The emergency preparedness industry has been booming for the last few years, and rightfully so. Have you taken your disaster prep seriously? If not, it's time to get prepared—the following list of items is perfect for any emergency kit.

Lighters. These products are commonly used in both high-tech and low-tech ways. You could use them to light an oil lamp or candle, start a campfire, or control sparks from flint and steel. These items should be kept in the house or car for your safety.

Flashlights. These products provide light at night and are often used for additions to camping gear. They can also be used in emergencies, such as when you are lost in the dark and need to find a way back home.

Batteries. Batteries are a necessity for various electronics, ranging from flashlights to radios.

Food. Food is necessary to live and survive during an emergency, so ensure that you have enough food on hand for your family's needs. Keep three to five days of food in your kit at all times, regardless of what the stores are selling.

Water. Ensure that you know how to purify water and making it healthy for drinking.

First-aid supplies. You should always have a first-aid kit on hand for any sort of emergencies that might occur, both large and small. Ensure that you can provide care for primary injuries such as stitches or burns.

Emergency medication. If necessary, you should also have enough medication on hand that can treat minor illnesses. This should include medicines such as painkillers and aspirin. Extra packing tape for both first-aid and medical use is also needed.

It's true—disasters have a way of sneaking up on us without warning, but it's never too early to get prepared!

Pack a backup just in case!

FOOD AND WATER STORAGE SURVIVAL GUIDE

Disasters happen. Natural disasters can strike without warning, catching people unprepared and destroying everything they cared about. Homes, schools, businesses, and lives are lost in an instant. Even though professionally planned emergencies rarely occur in a controlled environment like a lab or the safety of an office building, emergency response teams are always ready to help their communities when disaster strikes.

The best way to combat the chaos that could easily result from a natural disaster is with good preparation—both individual and community-wide practices will go a long way towards accomplishing this goal. Preparing ahead of time will help you keep you and your home safe.

Knowing how to store food and water in an emergency is an essential survival skill. As well, what if you decide to spend a weekend camping or you go on a multi-day business trip during winter? You'll need some of these storage ideas for sure!

We'll cover everything from what not to store your food in, how long foods last the best, and which foods are generally agreed-upon favorites. You can keep foods other than just grains, too, so don't worry if you aren't a fan. You can store things like:

Beans

Oats

Canned food. These foods are the easiest to use as they don't taste bad and lose their texture. Beans are high in protein, and oats make you feel full longer because of their high fiber content. Canned food is convenient as it heats up fast and doesn't require refrigeration for short-term storage. You can also purchase canned meats such as ham, chicken, or tuna fish.

- Popcorn for the holidays
- Canned beans or lentils
- Canned tuna fish (good for protein)

Vegetables. You can store these in a cool, dark place like your basement or an attic. Make sure you don't wash off the food before storing it, and keep the food appropriately sealed. They also contain different types of natural sugars and fiber.

- Potatoes
- Carrots
- Onions

You can store these foods in a cool, dry place such as your garage or basement. You'll want to keep food appropriately sealed and keep it out of direct sunlight or humidity. This list covers foods that are easy to cook, taste good, and have lots of protein. Many of them also have vitamin C in them, which helps with fighting off colds and illnesses.

Peanut butter

Cottage cheese

Hard-boiled eggs

HOW TO FIND WATER IN CASE OF DISASTER

SOS: We need water! As disasters become more common in our world, it's essential to know how to find potable water if you're ever stuck without it. Here are some ways to find water if you're ever in dire need.

1. Collect rainwater.

2. Collect dew.

3. Find a natural resource like a pond or stream.

4. Purify contaminated water by boiling it, adding Iodine tablets or drops, filtering with activated charcoal or sand filters, etc.

5. Know if water is safe to drink from these contaminated sources by using the "universal" precautions of avoiding water

that smells fetid, has an unusual color, or contains visible matter.

6. Use the sun to purify water.

7. Catch the condensation when you breathe on a container; this condensation will contain the vapor of your breath and be converted into drinking water.

8. If you're in a desert environment, dig for roots and tubers to survive. There's lots of moisture in these plants if you know where to look.

9. Make a watering can come out of a large canteen, and you can have water in an emergency.

10. Give your mouth a rinse and spit it into the container; this will help remove the taste of human waste from contaminated water.

11. Use gasoline to heat water, creating steam which can be converted into drinking water.

12. If you're in a disaster situation, sleep with your eyes open. You can search for food and water by moving your eyes across the horizon.

13. Eat the fruits, plants, and animals in your environment; they're full of water.

14. Use a battery-powered pump from a vehicle to produce pressure to produce drinking water from contaminated sources. This is also useful if you're in a hurricane or an earthquake situation where there might be damage throughout the area.

15. Soak logs in a bucket of water to create steam; you can then transfer it into bottles and use it as drinking water. Although it takes quite some time to produce steam, this method is inexpensive.

16. Boil salty water to remove the salt, making the water potable. You can then purify this water by using purification tablets.

17. Make sure that there's a heat source and an airtight container for this method; you can create a solar still to produce drinking water from contaminated sources.

18. Use a black garbage bag or tarp as a solar still; fill it up with water and position it to receive direct sunlight throughout the day.

19. Find clean sand and filter your contaminated water through it; this will remove bacteria and other contaminants from your water supply.

STORING AND PREPARING FOOD FOR DISASTERS

It is essential to be prepared for a disaster. That includes storing food so that it will last for the length of your emergency. It's also important to keep foods that are healthy and have a long shelf life.

This tells you how much food needs to be stored, how long-term storage works, and how you can prepare your food for emergencies. It also provides links with more information about disasters and what they do to the environment and instructions on what foods are best for different emergencies.

This is designed to give you some tips on how to store and prepare food for disasters.

1. When storing food, ensure that everything is secured tightly in plastic containers or zip-top bags to keep out moisture. Label everything with the date, so you know how old it is.

2. Don't forget about your freezer and refrigerator! If the electricity goes out during a disaster, you will want to use up your perishables before spoiling them.

3. Use oxygen absorbers to keep food from spoiling in buckets of emergency food buckets. You can also use Mylar bags. Some

food lasts for up to twenty-five years if packaged adequately with oxygen absorbers.

4. Opt for things like dried fruits and meats when you buy a new supply of emergency food. These last longer than canned goods, so they give you more bang for your buck. Keep these foods in airtight containers and rotate them regularly to ensure that the oldest items are used first.

5. If you have any pets, store enough pet food to last a minimum of eight weeks.

6. If you can use canned goods for your emergency food storage, you can use a pressure cooker for cooking up entire meals in one pot quickly. This will be useful if the power goes out and you are trying to cook on a camp stove. You can also opt to use slow-cookers that are very energy efficient and can be used on various fuel sources.

7. Pasta is cheap and filling, but it doesn't store very well or last long in emergency food scenarios because of its high starch content.

This is because nearly all survival experts agree that an emergency kit should include various nonperishable foods that can be stored without refrigeration.

It's also worth noting the importance of water, which should have its preparation steps in general, but is especially crucial for food. You need both enough water and enough food to keep you going throughout an emergency.

The following are some tips for storing and preparing food that you can use.

Planning Your Food Storage

Plans should include the number of people who will need to be fed in an emergency from your stored foods—don't just purchase as much food as possible for an emergency. You should consider the maximum number of people who need to be fed in an emergency and base your food storage plans on that instead. Planning on your family? Make extra food, because you know that some of them will never eat again. Planning on an entire town or city? Consider making extra food to be a complete catastrophe for the whole town/city if there are injuries or deaths during the disaster. You should also make sure that any emergency kit you purchase includes a variety of foods—your emergency kit should have a variety of foods. This is because it's unlikely that you'll encounter every type of food in an emergency; therefore, having a variety allows your family to be as prepared as possible. However, even if you're considering storing a variety of foods, don't go overboard. You should have enough food for a maximum number of people who you'll be feeding in an emergency. Once that's done, it's okay to purchase extra items, but make sure that you don't have enough food to feed the entire town. Preparing your stored food—whether you choose to keep dry or canned goods, regardless of which types of foods you choose to keep—proper preparation is crucial. If you're storing canned goods, make sure to rotate the cans every six months—rotating your canned goods is an easy way to ensure that your food stays fresh. Ensure that you keep track of what's new and are told not to eat any expired/expired food.

Food Item Storage

Everyone has food stored in their homes, but have you ever considered keeping your food for emergencies? I certainly didn't, but now I wish I had. Hurricanes happen all the time, and it's a terrible feeling to live through one and then realize that you lost a lot of your food supply because it was improperly stored or nondate able.

You should make a list of all the food that's in your pantry, grocery store, or anywhere else in your home. Make sure to know about all the snacks and other typical foods that are there too. After you've made a list, make sure you know how long it will last before it expires. You'd be very upset to come home and find out that you had nothing to eat.

After you've made a list of what you have, check it twice. Make sure that the food is not expired and that it isn't old. If you can't remember how long it's been there, look on the package for an expiration date. If there isn't one on the box, check your refrigerator or somewhere else to find out how long ago you bought it. If the date has passed, then throw the food away or donate it to a soup kitchen in your area.

After you've determined what you have and how long it'll last before it expires, you should determine what sort of food storage containers you will need. When people think of food storage, they often think about large containers such as five-gallon buckets. However, not all foods can be stored in these types of containers without going bad. For example, if you store sugar or flour without keeping it dry, the moisture will eventually go through the container and ruin the food within. Therefore, when deciding on a container for your food, don't forget about moisture proofing!

Book 8:

Preppers Cookbook

EDIBLE PLANTS

1. Alfalfa

Alfalfa is a wonderful diet for both horses and people. Alfalfa is nutrition dense. They were among the first to understand alfalfa, according to legend. These weeds may reach 3.5 feet tall with a deep root system. The stems have three-leaf clusters, like a clover. Many of these are located beside rivers, railways, abandoned farms, and meadows

2. Apple Blossom

Apple blooms are beautiful and delicious. They pair nicely with salads and desserts. Try some blooms over an apple pie with cream or in a cool glass of lemonade. Delicious, but take care. 1-2 blooms max per time. Too much may cause nausea.

3. Amaranth

Also called Amaranthus retroflexus. This weed is an edible plant found on most of the continents in work, but it is native to the Americas. All parts of this weed are edible, but you have to be careful because the leaves have spikes. Its leaves are spiky, but they are not poisonous. You can eat this weed raw if the conditions are really bad!

4. Artichoke

 The artichoke may grow up to 8 feet tall in sunny areas. The artichoke leaf is the most valued food component. This plant's lush greens are great for salads, stir-fries, and plain old supper sides. Artichoke roots have also been used to make various coffees and teas.

5. Asparagus

This vegetable is mostly found in Europe and North Africa, West Asia, and North America. The asparagus found in the wilderness has thinner stalks than the asparagus you find in the grocery stores. This plant is full of vitamin C & B6, potassium, and thiamine. You can eat it raw or boil it, whatever you like.

6. Baby's Breath

Baby's breath is a weed, yet it's beautiful, fragile blooms make it an attractive plant. This plant has a strong taproot and upright stalks. As the plant matures, the upright stem begins to sprawl. This plant produces tiny, beautiful white blooms with a green border.

7. Basil

You can use basil flowers as your alternative to leaves in a recipe that demands basil. Basil flowers should be used in moderation due to their strong flavor but can be added to many kinds of pasta, soups, or salad dishes.

8. Black Trumpet

Their form and color make these trumpet-shaped black mushrooms difficult to find. They resemble trumpet-shaped deadwood. The interior of these mushrooms is scaly and brittle. So, handle them with great care. These mushrooms have a strong stalk at the base and no gills. They develop in bunches.

9. Blackberry

Blackberry leaves may be palm or oval-shaped. The stems are robust and prickly, and the plants frequently yield excellent fruit that may be utilized in sweets, salads, jams, beverages, and wines. It is found in unmaintained wasteland, forest, and hedgerows.

10. Borage

Borage, or Borago Officinalis, is a common garden weed. Borage has long been considered to benefit the adrenal glands, kidneys, digestive system, and heart. In normal gardens, it protects pests like Japanese beetles and tomato worms from damaging other plants.

11. Broadleaf Plantain

This plant is high in nutrients, and you may use it medicinally to treat diarrhea and digestive problems. In a rosette, look for oval or egg-shaped leaves. When you break the stems, you'll discover strings that look like cereal. The leaves are edible.

12. Broccoli

In the wild, broccoli grows to a pretty good height, and the heads are seen sprouting up out of the plant. These plants grow nonstop for a few years straight, making them well within the parameters of a perennial plant. The entire broccoli plant is edible, making it the perfect food to forage.

13. Bull Thistle

Edible prickly weed unlike other thistles, the dark green leaf blades have a layer of short, prickly barbs. It's safe to eat even though it's rough to touch. The bull thistle is Cirsium Vulgare. Except for the flower, they can grow up to 3 feet tall.

14. Burdock

The leaves of Burdock are dark green on top and lighter, hairy underneath. The leaves are heart-shaped at the plant's base but thinner near the blossom stalk. After May, the stems turn woody, but fresh stems may be peeled and roasted. A tall stem develops when the plant is over a year old. The roots are lengthy and resemble black parsnips but grow in rocky soil, making harvesting difficult.

15. Calendula

Calendula officinalis is the scientific name for Pot Marigold. Marigolds have been grown for millennia, making their origin impossible to pinpoint. Leaves are oblong, toothed, and long. The leaf has thin hair-like features on both sides. The blooms are a brilliant yellow-orange. The petals are thick with a dark brown or black core. They like bright light and well-drained soil. The whole bloom may be eaten as a garnish. They may be candied and used as a garnish.

16. Carnations

The more fragrant the carnation, the more pronounced the taste. The majority of Dianthus species have a floral, clove-like flavor with a hint of spice. They are great for garnishing salads and soups and work well with sorbets, fruit salads, and ice cream. Only eat the petals, though, as the base of the flower has quite a bitter taste.

17. Catmint

These are small flowers characterized by a spicy and strong mint flavor. Thus they should be used in moderation. Add catmint to rice dishes into veggies and pasta dishes. You can also try these flowers to complement meat dishes.

18. Cattail

This plant was a part of the diets of different Native American tribes. Most parts of this plant are edible. You can eat the rootstocks or the rhizomes of Cattails. You can boil them or eat them raw. The best part of this plant is the white part of the stem that is near the bottom.

19. Chamomile

This is one of the most popular wild plants commonly harvested for its medicinal properties. This is believed to have a calming effect. Chamomile is believed to calm the nerves, ease digestive problems, help several skin conditions, and even reduce muscle spasms.

20. Chicken Mushrooms

This mushroom is a favorite among foragers and survivalists alike. These mushrooms may be as drab as the earth they grow on, but their vivid orange and yellow hues make them readily recognizable. Because of this, many beginner mushroom hunters think these mushrooms are toxic.

21. Chickweed

The garden wood is both applicable in medicine and diet. Whether raw or cooked, you can eat most weed parts, including the flowers, stems, and leaves. It tastes like spinach and incorporates well with many dishes.

22. Chicory

Cichorium intybus In Europe, North America, and Australia. This bushy shrub produces tiny blue, lavender, or white blooms. It can be eaten whole. Boil or consume the leaves uncooked. Boiling the roots makes them taste great. You can eat the flowers if you're craving a snack in the wilderness.

23. Clovers

Also called Trifolium. Clovers are edible plants. They can be found in any grassy area. It has trefoil leaflets which are how you identify this plant. Clovers can be eaten raw, but if you boil them, they would taste a lot better.

24. Coltsfoot

While the blossoms resemble dandelions, coltsfoot leaves have a waxy, heart-shaped appearance. The flowers, stems, and leaves are edible parts.

25. Common Chokecherry

This rose-like shrub is also a tree. Known as the red or eastern chokecherry. This plant's leaves alternate on the stalk. Each leaf is oval-shaped, long, and hairy at the tip. The leaves are darker towards the top of the tree and gradually lighter as you gaze downward.

26. Common Yarrow

The flowers and leaves of this plant are the only edible parts. They are rich in a variety of nutrients, but consuming too much of them is seldom advisable. When it comes to common yarrow, always opt for the flowers and young leaves. They have a slightly bitter taste when consumed raw.

27. Coriander

Coriander has thin, branching stems that may reach 3 feet. A pinnate leaflet grows from the stem to create the entire leaf. Upper leaves are thinner and more divided. Umbels of light purple and white blooms develop. Initially, the seeds appear as green berries. They become brown and fall off the plant as they ripen.

28. Cornflowers

These beautiful flowers can be used to add a touch of summer to omelets, pasta dishes, and salads. They mix well with other flowers and come in a variety of colors. The strength of flavor can differ slightly from flower to flower but range from a sweet to a spicy clove flavor.

29. Courgette

The majority of squash flowers have a sweet taste and thus can match well with cheese and other fillings. You can also butter courgette, deep fry, and sauté and add to pasta. Slice the flowers thinly and then add to scrambled eggs, omelets, soups, or just color your salads.

30. Crabapples

The crabapple is a common tree of the Malus genus. It blooms in white, pink, or rose. Its fruit is sour and yellow, orange, or red. This tree's leaves are oval with a pointed tip. In the spring, the leaves are green or dark green, and in the fall, they become orange or reddish-purple. The serrated leaves cluster.

31. Curly Dock

Yellow dock or curry dock's leaves may be eaten raw or cooked or added to soups and salads. You may eat the stem raw or cooked, roast, boil, or consume the uncooked ripe seeds. Its leaves are sour owing to high oxalic acid content; therefore, use caution. Also, replace the water often while cooking.

32. Damson Tree

The damson tree is a small to medium height tree and has oval leaves with a serrated edge. The leaves are shiny and dark green. They are sweet tasting and resemble a small plum. It can be found in woodlands, alongside pavements, in parks, and hedgerows

33. Dandelion

The weed normally grows anywhere, especially on grassy and in waste places. Its leaves normally grow from the base of the plant in a rosette, while its flower is developed from a hollow stalk. Dandelion normally produces a milky sap from its parts when cut out.

34. Daylily

Daylilies are adored by gardeners worldwide. Their beautiful flowers only last around 24 hours after blooming. The blooms bloom early in the morning and fade late at night. Abloom on the same stem sometimes replaces a wilted one. Some Lily species only bloom at night.

35. Dryads Saddle

The 8 cm long woody stem frequently darkens to black at the base. The underside of the cap contains huge irregularly shaped off-white pores. The crown is yellow to ochre and has a wide fan shape. It has dark brown scales. After a while, the inside flesh turns leathery. Found in deciduous trees.

36. Echinacea

Indigenous tribes of North America considered this medicinal herb incredibly helpful. It is believed to strengthen immunity levels, regulate blood sugar, control inflammation, and improve skin health. A tea made from echinacea leaves and its flower petals is said to have a calming effect.

37. Elderberry

This is an ornamental shrub and is quite popular in regular gardens. It's used to attract butterflies and a variety of birds. The only parts of this plant fit for consumption are the flowers and the berries.

38. Fennel

Fennel has long stalks that may reach 4 to 9 feet in height. They have big yellow flower clusters on top. Long feathery leaves with widely spread fronds. Its oblong, ribbed seeds the fragrance of fennel distinguishes it from other plants. Find it around roadsides, meadows, rocky slopes, and forest margins.

39. Field Blewit

The stem of these is off-white and has a blue/lilac covering. It is short, chunky, and swollen at the base. Cap underside is white to off white and busy. The cap is convex and of a beige to grey-brown color with white inner flesh. Found in meadows and grasslands, often grows in groups.

40. Fireweed

This plant is widespread throughout the US, although warmer regions like Texas and the Deep South may not be fortunate. The tall plant is called fireweed because it is typically the first item to sprout on the ground burned. Its vivid pink blooms easily identify it. It grows 3 to 6 feet tall. On a slope, you can see a field of fireweed.

41. Fuschia

These flowers serve as great green or fruit salad due to their shape, as they appear decorated if used into jerry when in crystals. Prepare the flower by removing the green and brown bits, and then remove the stamen pistils. Fuchsia berries are also edible and can be used to prepare jams.

42. Garland Chrysanthemum

Its leaves and blossoms are tasty. Or chrysanthemum leaves or tasty chrysanthemum leaves. It is rich in antioxidants and minerals but should never be eaten in excessive amounts. These flowers resemble daisies and have a variety of leaf forms. The petals are usually yellow in the middle, becoming white towards the end.

43. Giant Puffball Mushroom

The Puffball species of mushroom is indeed edible, but there are a few other kinds of mushrooms that mimic the appearance of the Puffball, which are not ideal mushrooms at all. The best way to know just what you are dealing with when it comes to these puffy kinds of mushrooms is to cut them open and look inside at the material.

44. Ground Plums

If you find ground plums sprouting off the vine, grab them! These resilient plums thrive all year with little inputs. They hang firmly in difficult terrains like dense woods and even mountain slopes. It's a delicious treat wherever you find it. Cooked or uncooked, these plums are tasty. Foraging for ground plums is rewarding.

45. Hairy Bittercress

Leaves grow opposite each other in pairs along the entire leave stem with one final leaf at the end. It grows close to the ground and has flowering stems which ground a little above the leaf height. Flowers are tiny and white and grow in small groups. Found in pathways, light grass, bare soil, and walls.

46. Hawthorn

Right at the outset of spring, the white flower petals of the Hawthorn plant begin to emerge. These eye-catching flowers are not only good to look at, however, but they are also very good to eat. The roughage of this plant makes for a great salad. And if you wait just a little while longer as spring begins to turn into summer, the berries that form on this plant can be collected and turned into a tasty, all-natural jelly for your toast!

47. Hedge Garlic

Hedge garlic has a two-year cycle. Its first year produces small, broadly heart-shaped leaves that are close to the ground. In its second year, the leaves become more triangular, and the leaf edges are serrated. The seeds, flowers, and leaves are all edible and work great in cooked foods and salads.

48. Hedgehog Fungus

Spines that may grow up to 6 mm long and range in color from white to pink salmon cover the gills and stem of this fungus. The stem is often off-center where it meets the caps. The cap is convex and uneven and occasionally has depressions around the center. It is a creamy yellow color or pale flesh/salmon-colored. It can be found in woodlands.

49. Hibiscus

The flower can be infused easily to prepare a citrus-tasting tea. Also, add a few strips of vibrantly colored petals to your fruits salads. However, only use the petals from flower heads as using the whole flower has plenty of pollen.

50. Kelp

Also called as Alaria esculenta. This is a seaweed found in almost all parts of the world. You can eat it raw. If you like, you can use it as an ingredient in your soup too. It is rich in vitamin K, lignans, and folate.

BREAKFAST

Banana and Prune Muffins

Serves: 12 / Preparation time: 10 minutes / Cooking time: 30 minutes

2 large bananas, peeled, mashed
8.8 ounces self-rising flour
14 ounces canned prunes, drained

1/8 teaspoon salt

1 teaspoon baking powder

1/2 teaspoon cinnamon

1 tablespoon castor sugar

1/2 teaspoon mixed spice

1/2 teaspoon baking soda

1 teaspoon vanilla extract, unsweetened

2.6 ounces butter, unsalted, softened

2 eggs

½ cup chopped walnuts

- Switch on the oven, then set it to 356 degrees F and let it preheat.
- Meanwhile, take a large bowl, and then place all the ingredients in it, reserving prunes, banana, and walnuts.
- Blend by using an immersion blender until smooth and then fold in banana and prunes until just mixed.
- Take a 12-cup muffin pan, grease with oil, fill evenly with the prepared batter and then top with walnuts.
- Bake for 30 minutes until muffins have thoroughly cooked and then remove muffins from cups.
- Let muffins cool for 10 minutes and then serve.

Per Serving: Calories: 200; Total Fat: 6.5 g; Saturated Fat: 3.5 g; Protein: 3.5 g; Carbs: 30.5 g; Fiber: 1 g; Sugar: 18 g

Rainbow Fruit Parfait

Serves: 4 / Preparation time: 5 minutes / Cooking time: 0 minutes

15 ounces canned sliced peaches, drained, diced
1 cup kiwi, peeled, diced
15 ounces canned cherries, drained
1 cup strawberries, hulled, diced
1 cup blackberries, quartered
3 cups granola
¼ cup mint leaves
4 cups vanilla Greek yogurt

Take a large glass, layer granola in its bottom, and then cover with some yogurt.

- Create layers by using some yogurt, some of the peach pieces, some more yogurt, some of the kiwi pieces, some more yogurt, some of the blackberry pieces, and remaining yogurt.
- Top with cherries, sprinkle with some granola and mint leaves, and then serve.

Per Serving: Calories: 110; Total Fat: 0.5 g; Saturated Fat: 0.1 g; Protein: 3 g; Carbs: 24 g; Fiber: 1 g; Sugar: 16 g

Breakfast Protein Bowl

Serves: 4 / Preparation time: 10 minutes / Cooking time: 0 minutes

14 ounces canned brown lentils, drained
1 zucchini, spiralized
5.6 ounces canned tuna pieces, packed in water or oil
1 avocado, peeled, destoned, sliced
¼ teaspoon salt
½ of lemon, juiced
2 eggs, boiled
For the dressing:
½ teaspoon minced garlic
2 teaspoons balsamic vinegar
1 tablespoon olive oil
For garnish:
2 teaspoons snipped chives
1 teaspoon black sesame seeds
2 teaspoons pumpkin seeds

- Prepare the dressing and for this, take a medium bowl, place all of its ingredients in it and whisk until combined.
- Add lentils and then stir until mixed.

- Spiralized zucchini, place it into a separate medium bowl, drizzle with lemon juice, season with salt and toss until coated.
- Peel the boiled eggs, cut them into slices, and arrange them into a large bowl.
- Arrange zucchini mixture, lentil mixture, avocado and tuna in portion into the bowl, sprinkle pumpkin seeds over zucchini, chives over lentils, and sesame seeds over eggs.
- Serve straight away.

Per Serving: Calories: 573; Total Fat: 34 g; Saturated Fat: 6.6 g; Protein: 37.3 g; Carbs: 24 g; Fiber: 11 g; Sugar: 3.2 g

Salmon and Pea Quiche

Serves: 4 / Preparation time: 10 minutes / Cooking time: 50 minutes

13.2 ounces of ready-to-rolled shortcrust pastry
6 ounces of canned salmon, skinless, boneless
10.5 ounces of canned garden peas
5 eggs, beaten
2/3 cup milk, semi-skimmed
Flour, as needed for dusting

2 tablespoons chopped chives

- Switch on the oven, then set it to 356 degrees F, place a 9-inch pie pan or quiche pan and let it preheat.
- Then carefully line the preheated pan with pastry, fill it with beans, and then bake for 10 minutes.
- After 10 minutes, remove beans from the pastry and then continue cooking for 10 minutes.
- Meanwhile, take a medium bowl, crack eggs in it and then whisk in milk until smooth.
- Add peas, salmon, and chives, and when after 10 minutes of baking, pour this mixture into pastry.
- Return pan into the oven and bake for 30 minutes until the filling has just set.
- Let quiche cool for 10 minutes, then cut it into slices and serve.

Per Serving: Calories: 638; Total Fat: 38 g; Saturated Fat: 14 g; Protein: 29 g; Carbs: 43 g; Fiber: 4 g; Sugar: 7 g

Breakfast Baked Eggs

Serves: 4 / Preparation time: 10 minutes / Cooking time: 20 minutes

14 ounces canned butterbeans, drained
1 medium white onion, peeled, sliced
13.4 ounces canned spinach, drained
14 ounces canned chopped tomatoes, drained
1 tablespoon dried mixed herbs
¼ teaspoon dried chili flakes
1 tablespoon olive oil
4 eggs
¼ cup of water
1 cube of vegetable stock
¼ cup chopped coriander

- Place a medium saucepan, place it over medium heat, add oil and when hot, add onion and cook for 5 minutes until soft.
- Add chili flakes and mixed herbs, stir until mixed and cook for 1 minute.
- Add tomatoes, then add the vegetable stock cube, crumble it, and then pour in water.

- Stir until combined, simmer the mixture for 5 minutes, then add spinach, beans, and mushrooms and simmer for 1 minute.
- Then make four wells in the mixture, crack an egg in each well, and cover the pan with lid.
- Cook for 3 to 5 minutes or until eggs have cooked to the desired level, and when done, sprinkle them with coriander.
- Serve eggs with toasted bread slices.

Per Serving: Calories: 199.9; Total Fat: 9.3 g; Saturated Fat: 3 g; Protein: 13.1 g; Carbs: 18 g; Fiber: 4.2 g; Sugar: 2.5 g

Oats with Fruit

Serves: 2 / Preparation time: 5 minutes / Cooking time: 0 minutes

½ of 14.4 ounces canned peach slices, packed in juice, drained
4 ounces oats
½ of 10.5 ounces canned mandarin segments, packed in juice, drained
¼ teaspoon cinnamon
½ cup milk, semi-skimmed
½ cup Greek yogurt

To Serve:
4 tablespoons granola

- Take a medium bowl, place all the ingredients in it, and then stir until combined.
- Cover the bowl with a lid and then refrigerate for a minimum of 8 hours.
- When ready to eat, divide oats and fruit evenly between two bowls, top with granola, and then serve.

Per Serving: Calories: 181; Total Fat: 3.1 g; Saturated Fat: 0.5 g; Protein: 5.1 g; Carbs: 34.8 g; Fiber: 6 g; Sugar: 6 g

Crust-less Quiche

Serves: 8 / Preparation time: 10 minutes / Cooking time: 30 minutes

1/2 cup diced deli ham
4 ounces canned sliced mushrooms, drained
1/2 of 14.5 ounces canned chopped tomatoes, drained
1/2 cup chopped scallions
½ teaspoon salt
¼ teaspoon ground black pepper
2 teaspoons cornstarch

1 teaspoon dried mustard

4 eggs

1/2 cup grated parmesan cheese

1 cup grated cheddar cheese

1 1/3 cups milk, unsweetened

1 ½ cups croutons

- Switch on the oven, then set it to 375 degrees F and let it preheat.
- In the meantime, take a large bowl, crack eggs in it, add mustard and cornstarch, pour in the milk, and whisk until blended.
- Add mushroom, scallion, and ham, tomatoes, salt, and black pepper, stir until mixed and spoon the mixture into a quiche dish or a 9-inch pie plate.
- Top the mixture with cheeses and crouton and then bake for 30 minutes until set and cooked.
- When done, let quiche cool on a wire rack for 15 minutes, then cut it into slices and serve.

Per Serving: Calories: 180; Total Fat: 9 g; Saturated Fat: 4.5 g; Protein: 14 g; Carbs: 11 g; Fiber: 1 g; Sugar: 4 g

Spinach, Chickpea and Potato Hash

Serves: 4 / Preparation time: 10 minutes / Cooking time: 18 minutes

1 can of diced potatoes, drained
1 medium white onion, peeled, sliced
1/2 can of chopped tomatoes
½ teaspoon salt
1/2 can of chickpeas
¼ teaspoon ground black pepper
1 can of spinach, drained
1 teaspoon curry powder
2 tablespoons olive oil
4 eggs
1 tablespoon chopped parsley

- Place a large frying pan, place it over medium heat, add oil and when hot, add onion and cook for 5 minutes until soft.
- Stir in curry powder, then add potatoes, switch heat to medium-high level, and then cook for 5 minutes until onion begins to brown.
- Add spinach and tomatoes, season with salt and black pepper and continue cooking for 3 minutes until hot.

- Meanwhile, take a frying pan, place it over medium heat, add oil for frying eggs and when hot, crack the egg in it and cook until fried to the desired level.
- When potato mixture has cooked, divide it evenly among plates, top with a fried egg, and then serve.

Per Serving: Calories: 382; Total Fat: 20 g; Saturated Fat: 7 g; Protein: 14 g; Carbs: 37 g; Fiber: 7 g; Sugar: 3 g

Tropical Muffins

Serves: 12 / Preparation time: 10 minutes / Cooking time: 25 minutes

8 ounces canned crushed pineapple, drained
1 1/2 cups all-purpose flour
1/2 teaspoon salt
1 teaspoon baking powder
1/2 cup sugar
1/4 cup butter, unsalted, softened
1/2 teaspoon baking soda
1 1/2 teaspoons rum extract
1/2 cup shredded coconut, sweetened
1/3 cup chopped pecans
1 egg

1 cup sour cream

- Switch on the oven, then set it to 375 degrees F and let it preheat.
- Meanwhile, take a large bowl, place butter in it, and then beat in sugar until fluffy.
- Then beat in egg, rum extract, and sour cream until combined.
- Take a medium bowl, place flour in it, and then stir in salt, baking powder, and soda until mixed.
- Gradually stir flour mixture into the egg mixture and then fold in pecans, coconut and pineapple until incorporated.
- Take a 12-cup muffin pan, line cups with muffin cups, fill them evenly with prepared batter and then bake for 25 minutes until thoroughly cooked.
- When done, remove muffins from pan, let them cool for 10 minutes and then serve.

Per Serving: Calories: 225; Total Fat: 11 g; Saturated Fat: 6 g; Protein: 3 g; Carbs: 26 g; Fiber: 1 g; Sugar: 13 g

Oats with Fruits and Coconut Milk

Serves: 4 / Preparation time: 5 minutes / Cooking time: 0 minutes

2 cups rolled oats, old-fashioned
15 ounces canned tropical fruit salad, drained
½ teaspoon ground ginger
1/8 teaspoon salt
13.5 ounces canned coconut milk, unsweetened
Toasted almonds as needed for serving

- Take a medium bowl, place oats in it, add ginger and salt, and then pour in the milk.
- Stir until mixed, cover the bowl and then let it refrigerate for a minimum of 8 hours or until oats have turned tender.
- When ready to eat, stir the oats, divide evenly among bowls and then top with fruit salad and almonds.
- Serve straight away.

Per Serving: Calories: 440; Total Fat: 26 g; Saturated Fat: 19 g; Protein: 8 g; Carbs: 49 g; Fiber: 5 g; Sugar: 18 g

All-Day Breakfast

Serves: 4 / Preparation time: 10 minutes / Cooking time: 20 minutes

8.8 ounces firm tofu, drained
14.6 ounces canned baked beans
¼ cup snipped chives
19.7 ounces canned whole potatoes, drained
10.5 ounces canned whole tomatoes, drained
¼ cup chopped parsley
10.2 ounces canned sliced mushrooms, drained
1 teaspoon garlic powder
1 teaspoon ground black pepper
½ teaspoon smoked paprika
½ teaspoon dried thyme
2 teaspoon barbecue seasoning mix
1 tablespoon cornflakes, crushed
2 tablespoons olive oil
1 avocado, peeled, destoned, sliced

- Take a grill pan, place it over high heat, grease it lightly with oil and let it preheat.
- Meanwhile, take a shallow dish, place cornflakes in it, add barbecue seasoning mix, and stir until mixed.

- Cut tofu into small pieces, and then coat them evenly with cornflake mixture.
- Transfer tofu pieces to the grill pan, drizzle with oil, and then grill for 4 minutes per side.
- In the meantime, slice the whole potatoes and then sprinkle with black pepper, garlic powder, chives, and parsley.
- Transfer potatoes to the grill pan and grill for 5 minutes per side until crisp.
- Take a medium bowl, add mushrooms in it along with tomatoes, sprinkle with paprika and toss until coat.
- Transfer mushrooms and tomatoes to the grill pan and grill for 3 minutes per side until hot.
- Divide tofu and grilled vegetables evenly among plates and then serve evenly with avocado and baked beans.

Per Serving: Calories: 646; Total Fat: 25.5 g; Saturated Fat: 5 g; Protein: 35.1 g; Carbs: 60 g; Fiber: 17.7 g; Sugar: 11.8 g

Citrus Cornmeal Cake

Serves: 8 / Preparation time: 10 minutes / Cooking time: 20 minutes

15 ounces canned mandarin oranges, packed in juiced, drained

3/4 cup all-purpose flour
1 teaspoon baking powder
1/2 cup cornmeal
1/2 teaspoon grated orange zest
3 tablespoons sliced almonds
1/4 teaspoon almond extract, unsweetened
1/3 cup honey
1/4 cup olive oil
1/2 cup lemon yogurt
1 egg
2 egg whites

- Switch on the oven, then set it to 350 degrees F and let it preheat.
- Take a large bowl, add egg and egg white in it and then beat in oil, honey, and yogurt until well blended.
- Take a medium bowl, place flour, baking powder, and cornmeal in it and stir until mixed.
- Gradually beat flour mixture into the egg mixture until incorporated and then beat in orange zest until mixed.
- Take a 9-inches tart pan with a removable bottom, grease with cooking spray, pour in the prepared batter and then top with orange and almonds.
- Bake for 30 minutes until cooked through, and when done, cool the cake for 10 minutes.
- Cut cake into slices and then serve.

Per Serving: Calories: 240; Total Fat: 9 g; Saturated Fat: 1 g; Protein: 5 g; Carbs: 36 g; Fiber: 2 g; Sugar: 20 g

Peach Pancakes

Serves: 4 / Preparation time: 5 minutes / Cooking time: 15 minutes

4.75 ounces flour
14.6 ounces canned peach slices, packed in syrup, drained
1/2 teaspoon salt
1 teaspoon baking powder
2 tablespoons caster sugar
1 teaspoon maple syrup
2 tablespoons melted butter, unsalted
1 egg, beaten
½ cup milk, unsweetened
Icing sugar to dust

- Take a large bowl, place all the ingredients in it except for peaches, maple syrup and icing sugar and then blend by using an immersion blender until smooth.

- Take a medium skillet pan, place it over medium heat, add some oil to grease the pan, and when hot, drop batter in it until pan gets full.
- Spread the mixture to shape pancakes and then cook for 4 minutes per side until nicely browned and cooked.
- When done, top pancakes with peach slices, drizzle with maple syrup, sprinkle with icing sugar, and then serve.

Per Serving: Calories: 321; Total Fat: 11 g; Saturated Fat: 5 g; Protein: 7 g; Carbs: 47 g; Fiber: 2 g; Sugar: 20.5 g

Chili Cornbread Muffins

Serves: 18 / Preparation time: 10 minutes / Cooking time: 20 minutes
For the Cornbread:
14.75 ounces canned cream-style sweet corn
2 cups yellow cornmeal
14.75 ounces canned sweet corn kernel, drained
1/2 teaspoon salt
1/2 teaspoon baking soda
2/3 cup sugar
1/2 cup unsalted butter, melted
2 eggs

1 cup evaporated milk, canned
For the Chili:
6 chili with beans from 15 oz. can, drained, warmed
Sour cream as needed for topping

- Switch on the oven, then set it to 375 degrees F and let it preheat.
- Take a large bowl, crack eggs in it, add butter and sugar, pour in the milk, and whisk until smooth.
- Add salt and baking soda and then fold in cream-style corn, cornmeal, and sweet corn until incorporated.
- Take one and half 12 cups muffin pan, grease each cup with oil and then evenly fill with the prepared batter.
- Bake for 15 to 20 minutes until muffins have thoroughly cooked and then let cool for 10 minutes.
- Remove muffins from pan, then cut out the center from each muffin by using a small knife and fill evenly with chili.
- Top muffins with sour cream and then serve.

Per Serving: Calories: 310; Total Fat: 14 g; Saturated Fat: 7 g; Protein: 10 g; Carbs: 36 g; Fiber: 2 g; Sugar: 14 g

LUNCH

Vegetable Pot Pie

Serves: 6 / Preparation time: 10 minutes / Cooking time: 30 minutes

2 tablespoons all-purpose flour
2 tablespoons unsalted butter
3 cups frozen mixed vegetables, thawed
15-ounces canned lentils, drained

1/2 teaspoon salt

1 teaspoon French four spice

1 tablespoon Dijon mustard

1 tablespoon olive oil

1 sheet of pie crust, refrigerated

1 cup vegetable broth

1/4 cup grated Parmesan cheese

- Switch on the oven, then set it to 375 degrees F and let it preheat.
- Meanwhile, take a large skillet pan, place it over medium heat, add butter and when it melts, add lentils and mixed vegetables and then cook for 5 minutes until thoroughly heated.
- Then stir in flour, whisk in broth until blended and bring the mixture to a boil, stirring continuously.
- Switch heat to medium heat, simmer the mixture for 1 to 2 minutes until thickened and then stir in salt, four spice, and mustard.
- Take a 9-in pie plate, grease it with oil, pour in the cooked filling and then cover with pie crust, trimming the edges and make slits in the center.
- Brush the crust with oil, sprinkle with cheese and then bake for 30 minutes until crust has turned nicely golden brown.
- When done, cool the pie for 5 minutes and then serve.

Per Serving: Calories: 356; Total Fat: 17 g; Saturated Fat: 7 g; Protein: 10 g; Carbs: 41 g; Fiber: 9 g; Sugar: 5 g

Hamburger Soup

Serves: 8 / Preparation time: 10 minutes / Cooking time: 40 minutes

1 pound ground beef
1 medium white onion, peeled, chopped
3 medium carrots, sliced
2 medium potatoes, peeled and cubed
1 cup of frozen green beans
14.5-ounces canned of diced tomatoes, undrained
1/2 cup chopped celery
1 ½ teaspoons salt
¼ teaspoon ground black pepper
¼ teaspoon dried oregano
4 teaspoons beef bouillon granules
4 cups of water

- Place a large saucepan, place it over medium heat and when hot, add beef and cook for 5 to 8 minutes until brown.
- Drain the excess grease from the pan, then add remaining ingredients except for beans and oregano, stir until mixed, and bring it to a boil.
- Then switch heat to medium-low level and simmer the soup for 15 minutes until vegetables have turned tender.
- Add green beans, cover the pan and simmer for 15 minutes until beans have turned tender.
- When done, ladle soup into bowls, garnish with oregano and then serve.

Per Serving: Calories: 178; Total Fat: 7 g; Saturated Fat: 3 g; Protein: 13 g; Carbs: 15 g; Fiber: 3 g; Sugar: 5 g

Cheeseburger Pasta

Serves: 4 / Preparation time: 10 minutes / Cooking time: 15 minutes

3/4 pound ground beef
2 tablespoons chopped white onion
2 tablespoons dill pickle relish

2 green onions, chopped

14.5-ounces canned diced tomatoes, no-salt-added

2 tablespoons mustard paste

1/4 teaspoon seasoned salt

1 teaspoon steak seasoning

1 tablespoon olive oil

2 tablespoons ketchup

1 1/2 cups penne pasta, cooked

3/4 cup shredded cheddar cheese

- Place a large skillet pan, place it over medium heat, add oil and when hot, add onion and beef and then cook for 5 to 8 minutes until beef is no longer pink.
- Drain the excess fat, add cooked pasta, add remaining ingredients except for cheese and green onions and bring the mixture to a boil.
- Then switch heat to medium-low level and simmer for 5 minutes.
- After 5 minutes, remove the pan from heat, add cheese, cover the pan and let it stand for 5 minutes until cheese melts.
- Garnish pasta with green onions and then serve.

Per Serving: Calories: 391; Total Fat: 12 g; Saturated Fat: 6 g; Protein: 28 g; Carbs: 43 g; Fiber: 4 g; Sugar: 10 g

Mixed Vegetable Soup

Serves: 2 / Preparation time: 10 minutes / Cooking time: 20 minutes

14.5-ounces canned diced tomatoes, undrained
1/2 of a small carrot, grated
2 tablespoons chopped green bell pepper
1/2 of a celery rib, chopped
1 tablespoon chopped green onion
1/8 teaspoon ground black pepper
3/4 teaspoon sugar
1 tablespoon butter, unsalted
1 cup chicken broth, divided
1 1/2 teaspoons cornstarch

- Take a small saucepan, place it over medium heat, add butter and when it melts, add onion, green pepper, celery, and carrot and cook for 5 to 7 minutes until tender.
- Reserve 2 tablespoons of broth, pour remaining broth into the pan, add tomato, black pepper, and sugar and then bring it to a boil.
- Then switch heat to medium-low level, cover the pan and simmer the soap for 10 minutes.

- Stir together reserved broth and cornstarch, add to the soap, stir until smooth and bring it to a boil.
- Then cook soap for 2 minutes until slightly thickened and serve.

Per Serving: Calories: 124; Total Fat: 6 g; Saturated Fat: 4 g; Protein: 4 g; Carbs: 16 g; Fiber: 4 g; Sugar: 10 g

Black Bean Veggie Burgers

Serves: 4 / Preparation time: 10 minutes / Cooking time: 20 minutes

½ of medium white onion, peeled, cut into wedges
16-ounces canned black beans, drained
½ of green bell pepper, cored, 2-inch diced
1 ½ teaspoon minced garlic
1 tablespoon cumin
1 tablespoon red chili powder
1 teaspoon hot sauce
1 egg
½ cup bread crumbs

- Switch on the oven, then set it to 375 degrees F and let it preheat.

- Take a medium bowl, place beans in it, and then mash them with a fork until thick mixture comes together.
- Place onions in a food processor, add bell pepper and garlic, and pulse for 1 to 2 minutes until finely chopped.
- Add the mixture into the black beans mixture and then stir until well combined.
- Take a small bowl, crack the egg in it, add cumin, red chili powder, and hot sauce and whisk until frothy.
- Add egg mixture into the black beans mixture along with bread crumbs and then stir until sticky mixture comes together.
- Shape the mixture into four patties and then arrange them on a grease baking sheet.
- Bake the black beans patties for 10 minutes per side and then serve.

Per Serving: Calories: 198; Total Fat: 3 g; Saturated Fat: 1 g; Protein: 11.2 g; Carbs: 33.1 g; Fiber: 9.8 g; Sugar: 2 g

Pineapple Meatballs

Serves: 24 / Preparation time: 10 minutes / Cooking time: 25 minutes

8 ounces canned crushed pineapple

1/2 pound pork sausage

1/2 pound ground beef

1/4 cup dry bread crumbs

1/8 teaspoon ground black pepper

1 egg

For the Glaze:

2 tablespoons Dijon and mayonnaise blend

1/4 cup white vinegar

1/4 cup ketchup

1/4 cup brown sugar

1/4 cup water

- Switch on the oven, then set it to 450 degrees F and let it preheat.
- Reserve the juice of pineapple, and then place crushed pineapple into a large bowl.
- Drizzle with 2 tablespoons of pineapple juice, add beef, sausage, black pepper, bread crumbs, and eggs and stir until well mixed.
- Shape the mixture into 1-inch meatballs, arrange them into a greased baking pan and then bake for 15 minutes until the internal temperature of meatballs reaches 160 degrees F.
- Meanwhile, take a large skillet pan, place it over medium heat, pour in reserved pineapple juice, add all

the ingredients for the glaze and then cook for 2 to 4 minutes until hot, set aside until required.

- Then add baked meatballs into the skillet pan containing glaze, toss until coated, and bring to a boil.
- Switch heat to the low level and continue cooking for 5 minutes or until hot.
- Serve straight away.

Per Serving: Calories: 66; Total Fat: 3 g; Saturated Fat: 1 g; Protein: 3 g; Carbs: 5 g; Fiber: 0 g; Sugar: 4 g

Greek Chicken Salad

Serves: 6 / Preparation time: 10 minutes / Cooking time: 0 minutes

For the Salad:
14-ounces canned butterbeans, packed in water, drained
30 black olives, pitted
12-ounces canned chicken, drained, shredded
14-ounces canned kidney beans, packed in water, drained
7-ounces cherry tomatoes, halved
½ of a medium cucumber, diced
½ cup chopped parsley
For the dressing:

1/8 teaspoon salt

1 teaspoon dried oregano

1/8 teaspoon ground black pepper

1 teaspoon mustard

2 tablespoons honey

4 tablespoons lemon juice

6 tablespoons olive oil

For Serving:

½ cup mint leaves

4.4-ounces crumbled feta cheese

8.4-ounces mixed salad leaves

- Take a large bowl, place all the ingredients for the salad in it and then stir until mixed.
- Prepare the dressing, and for this, take a jam jar, place all the ingredients for the dressing in it, cover with the lid and shake well.
- Add the dressing into the salad, toss until coated, and then taste to adjust seasoning.
- Serve the salad and for this, take a large plate, layer its bottom with salad leaves, top with prepared salad and then top with cheese and mint leaves.
- Serve straight away.

Per Serving: Calories: 380; Total Fat: 19.5 g; Saturated Fat: 5.5 g; Protein: 27.5 g; Carbs: 20 g; Fiber: 7.5 g; Sugar: 9.5 g

Pasta Fagioli

Serves: 12 / Preparation time: 10 minutes / Cooking time: 55 minutes

4 ounces pasta shells, uncooked
1 pound ground beef
7.5 ounces canned cannellini beans, drained
4 celery ribs, diced
28-ounces canned diced tomatoes, undrained
8 ounces canned kidney beans, drained
2 medium white onions, peeled, chopped
1 ½ medium carrots, peeled, sliced
1 ½ teaspoon ground black pepper
½ teaspoon dried oregano
¾ teaspoon hot pepper sauce
1 ½ can of beef broth, each about 14.5-ounces
26-ounces canned spaghetti sauce
3 teaspoons minced parsley

- Place a large pot, place it over medium heat and when hot, add beef and cook for 5 to 8 minutes until beef is no longer pink.
- Drain the excess fat, add remaining ingredients, reserving pasta and parsley, stir until mixed, and then bring the mixture to a boil.

- Switch heat to medium-low level and simmer for 30 minutes until cooked, covering the pot.
- Add parsley and pasta and then continue simmering for 10 to 14 minutes until pasta has turned soft, covering the pot.
- Serve straight away.

Per Serving: Calories: 212; Total Fat: 6 g; Saturated Fat: 2 g; Protein: 14 g; Carbs: 25 g; Fiber: 5 g; Sugar: 8 g

Jalapeno Mac and Cheese

Serves: 15 / Preparation time: 20 minutes / Cooking time: 3 hours

4 jalapeno peppers, deseeded, chopped
16-ounces elbow macaroni, uncooked
1/4 teaspoon ground bell pepper
10.75-ounces canned cream of onion soup, condensed, undiluted
3 cups shredded cheddar cheese
10.75-ounces canned cheddar cheese soup, condensed, undiluted
6 tablespoons butter, unsalted, divided
2 cups whole milk, unsweetened

1/2 cup mayonnaise

2 cups shredded Colby-Monterey Jack cheese

1 cup crushed Ritz crackers

- Place a large skillet pan, place it over medium-high heat, add 2 tablespoons of butter and when it melts, add jalapeno and cook for 5 minutes until tender-crisp.
- Transfer jalapeno with butter into a slow cooker, add remaining ingredients except for remaining butter and cracker, and shut with lid.
- Plugin the slow cooker and then cook for 3 hours at a low heat setting until cooked through.
- When done, place a frying pan, add butter in it, wait until it melts, stir in crackers and remove the pan from heat.
- Spread cracker mixture over the macaroni and then serve.

Per Serving: Calories: 428; Total Fat: 27 g; Saturated Fat: 13 g; Protein: 14 g; Carbs: 33 g; Fiber: 2 g; Sugar: 5 g

Salmon Fishcakes

Serves: 4 / Preparation time: 10 minutes / Cooking time: 6 minutes

10-ounces canned peas, drained
½ bunch of chives, chopped
1-ounces canned potatoes, drained
1 tablespoon flour, and more for dusting
12-ounces canned salmon, drained
1/3 teaspoon salt
¼ teaspoon ground black pepper
1 lemon, juiced
2 tablespoons olive oil
1 egg

- Take a medium bowl, place potatoes in it, mash them and then mash in peas and salmon until combined.
- Add eggs, lemon juice, chives, salt, and black pepper, stir until well mixed and then shape the mixture into four patties.
- Take a medium skillet pan, place it over medium heat, add oil and when hot, add patties and cook for 3 minutes per side until nicely browned and thoroughly cooked.
- Serve straight away.

Per Serving: Calories: 167; Total Fat: 6.3 g; Saturated Fat: 2 g; Protein: 11.7 g; Carbs: 15.3 g; Fiber: 1 g; Sugar: 2 g

Red Pepper Chicken

Serves: 4 / Preparation time: 15 minutes / Cooking time: 6 hours

4 chicken breast halves, each about 4 ounces
1 large white onion, peeled, chopped
15-ounces canned black beans, no-salt-added, drained
12-ounces jarred roasted sweet red peppers, drained, cut into strips
14.5-ounces canned Mexican stewed tomatoes, undrained
¼ teaspoon ground black pepper
White rice, cooked, for serving

- Switch on a slow cooker, grease it lightly with oil and then place chicken in it.
- Take a medium mixing bowl, place onion, pepper, red pepper, tomatoes, and beans in it and then stir until mixed.
- Spread bean mixture over chicken, shut with the lid, and cook for 6 hours at a low heating setting.

- When done, serve chicken and peppers over cooked rice.

Per Serving: Calories: 288; Total Fat: 3 g; Saturated Fat: 1 g; Protein: 30 g; Carbs: 28 g; Fiber: 7 g; Sugar: 8 g

Fish Tacos

Serves: 4 / Preparation time: 10 minutes / Cooking time: 20 minutes

14.7 ounces canned salmon, drained
14 ounces canned cannellini beans, drained
8 spring onions, thinly sliced
6 ounces canned sweetcorn, drained
2 heads of lettuce
4.4 ounces canned mackerel, drained
4 tablespoons chopped coriander
½ teaspoon minced garlic
2 tablespoons Siracha sauce
¼ teaspoon lemon juice
4 tablespoons olive oil
7 ounces mayonnaise
8 tacos

- Take a medium skillet pan, place it over medium heat, add oil and when hot, add onion and garlic, and cook for 5 minutes until soft.
- Add beans, stir until mixed and continue cooking for 2 minutes until thoroughly warmed.
- Remove pan from heat, transfer bean mixture into a medium bowl, break it by using a fork and then stir in mayonnaise until combined.
- Cut the fish into bite-size pieces, add to the mayonnaise mixture, drizzle with lemon juice and fold until just mixed.
- Divide the mixture evenly among tortilla, top with lettuce and coriander and then drizzle with Sriracha sauce.
- Fold the tortillas and then serve.

Per Serving: Calories: 244; Total Fat: 12 g; Saturated Fat: 4.1 g; Protein: 16 g; Carbs: 18 g; Fiber: 1.5 g; Sugar: 1.4 g

Spicy Goulash

Serves: 12 / Preparation time: 10 minutes / Cooking time: 6 hours and 30 minutes

2 cups elbow macaroni, uncooked
1 medium white onion, peeled, chopped
1 pound ground beef
2 cans of kidney beans, each about 16-ounces, drained
1 medium green pepper, cored, chopped
4 cans of Mexican diced tomatoes, each about 14.5-ounces, undrained
1/4 teaspoon ground black pepper
1 teaspoon dried basil
1 teaspoon ground cumin
1 teaspoon dried parsley flakes
2 tablespoons red chili powder
1/4 cup red wine vinegar
1 tablespoon Worcestershire sauce
2 teaspoons beef bouillon granules
2 cups of water

- Place a large skillet pan, place it over medium heat, and when hot, add beef and cook for 5 to 8 minutes until beef is no longer pink.

- Drain the excess grease, transfer beef into a slow cooker and then add remaining ingredients except for macaroni.
- Plugin the slow cooker, shut it with the lid, and then cook for 6 hours at low heat setting until thoroughly heated.
- Then stir in the macaroni, shut with the lid, and continue cooking for 30 minutes or longer until tender.
- Serve straight away.

Per Serving: Calories: 222; Total Fat: 5 g; Saturated Fat: 2 g; Protein: 15 g; Carbs: 30 g; Fiber: 6 g; Sugar: 7 g

Salmon and Bean Salad

Serves: 4 / Preparation time: 10 minutes / Cooking time: 0 minutes

For the salad:
1 pouch of ready-to-cook couscous
1 can of pink salmon, packed in water, drained
1/2 of a medium cucumber, diced
1 can of sweetcorn, drained
10 cherry tomatoes, quartered
1 can of haricot beans, drained

2 ounces baby spinach

For the dressing:

¼ teaspoon salt

¼ teaspoon ground black pepper

1/8 dried chili flakes

1 teaspoon honey

¼ cup white wine vinegar

½ cup rapeseed oil

- Prepare the dressing and for this, take a jam jar, add all of its ingredients in it, shut with the lid and then shake well until combined.
- Take a large bowl, place all the ingredients for the salad in it, and toss until well mixed.
- Divide salad evenly among plates, drizzle with prepared salad dressing and then serve.

Per Serving: Calories: 272.6; Total Fat: 8.7 g; Saturated Fat: 2 g; Protein: 25.5 g; Carbs: 23 g; Fiber: 6.5 g; Sugar: 1 g

DINNER

Lemony Greek Beef and Vegetables

Serves: 4 / Preparation time: 10 minutes / Cooking time: 20 minutes

1 can of navy beans, about 16 ounces, drained
1 pound ground beef
5 medium carrots, peeled, sliced

1 bunch of baby bok choy, trimmed

1 ½ tablespoon minced garlic

1/4 cup and 2 tablespoons white wine, divided

1/4 teaspoon salt

2 teaspoons dried oregano

2 tablespoons lemon juice

1 tablespoon olive oil

1/2 cup shredded Parmesan cheese

- Prepare the bok choy, and for this, chop its leaves and then cut its stalks into 1-inch pieces.
- Place a large skillet pan, place it over medium-high heat, and when hot, add beef and cook for 5 to 7 minutes until nicely browned.
- Drain the excess grease, transfer beef to a bowl, add oil and when hot, add stalks of bok choy and carrots and cook for 5 to 7 minutes until tender-crisp.
- Stir in leaves of bok choy, and garlic, pour in ¼ cup of wine, then switch heat to medium-high level and cook for 5 minutes until nicely browned.
- Return beef into the pan, add remaining ingredients except for lemon juice and cheese, and stir until mixed.
- Switch heat to medium-low level, simmer for 3 minutes and then remove the pan from heat.
- Drizzle with lemon juice, sprinkle with cheese and then serve.

Per Serving: Calories: 478; Total Fat: 21 g; Saturated Fat: 7 g; Protein: 36 g; Carbs: 36 g; Fiber: 10 g; Sugar: 7 g

Cream of Turkey and Wild Rice Soup

Serves: 6 / Preparation time: 10 minutes / Cooking time: 20 minutes

2 cups diced cooked turkey
1 medium white onion, peeled, chopped
1 can of sliced mushrooms, about 4 ounces, drained
6 ounces of long grain and wild rice mix with seasoning
1 tablespoon minced parsley
2 tablespoons butter, unsalted
2 cups chicken broth
3 cups of water
1 cup heavy whipping cream

- Place a large saucepan, place it over medium heat, add butter and when it melts, add onion and mushrooms and then cook for 5 minutes until tender.
- Add rice mix along with seasoning, pour in broth and water, stir until mixed and bring the mixture to a boil.

- Then switch heat to medium-low level and simmer for 20 minutes until rice has turned tender.
- Add turkey and cream, stir until mixed and cook for 5 minutes until thoroughly heated.
- Garnish with minced parsley and then serve.

Per Serving: Calories: 364; Total Fat: 21 g; Saturated Fat: 12 g; Protein: 19 g; Carbs: 25 g; Fiber: 1 g; Sugar: 3 g

Meatball Soup

Serves: 6 / Preparation time: 10 minutes / Cooking time: 35 minutes

36 meatballs
1 can of cannellini beans, about 15 ounces, drained
2 celery ribs, chopped
1 small white onion, peeled, chopped
3/4 cup canned green beans cut
15 baby carrots, chopped
1 can of Italian diced tomatoes, about 14.5ounces, undrained
3/4 cup chopped cabbage
¼ teaspoon salt
¼ teaspoon paprika
¼ teaspoon ground black pepper
1 teaspoon Italian seasoning

4 teaspoons olive oil, divided

1 can of chicken broth, about 14.5 ounces

3 tablespoons shredded mozzarella cheese

- Place a large skillet pan, place it over medium heat, add 2 teaspoons oil and when hot, add meatballs and cook for 3 to 4 minutes per side until browned, set aside until required.
- Take a large saucepan, place it over medium heat, add remaining oil and when hot, add onion, carrot, and celery and cook for 5 to 8 minutes until tender.
- Add tomatoes, cabbage, green beans, and cannellini beans, pour in the broth, season with salt, black pepper, paprika, and Italian seasoning and bring the mixture to a boil.
- Switch heat to medium-low level, add meatballs and simmer for 20 minutes until beans have turned tender.
- Sprinkle with cheese, wait until it melts, and then serve the soup.

Per Serving: Calories: 254; Total Fat: 10 g; Saturated Fat: 2 g; Protein: 19 g; Carbs: 21 g; Fiber: 5 g; Sugar: 7 g

Baked Ham with Pineapple

Serves: 20 / Preparation time: 10 minutes / Cooking time: 2 hours

1 fully cooked ham, bone-in, about 8 pounds
1 can of sliced pineapple, about 20 ounces
12 maraschino cherries
Whole cloves as needed
1/2 cup brown sugar

- Switch on the oven, then set it to 325 degrees F and let it preheat.
- Meanwhile, take a roasting pan, place ham in it, use a sharp to score diamond shape cuts on its surface, and then insert cloves in those cuts.
- Cover with foil and then bake the ham for 1 hour and 30 minutes.
- Reserve ¼ cup of juice from the pineapple, add sugar into the juice, stir until mixed and pour it over baked ham.
- Arrange cherries and pineapple slices on ham and continue baking for 45 minutes until the internal temperature of the ham reaches 140 degrees F.
- Serve straight away.

Per Serving: Calories: 219; Total Fat: 13 g; Saturated Fat: 5 g; Protein: 17 g; Carbs: 8 g; Fiber: 0 g; Sugar: 8 g

Pineapple Jerk Chicken and Rice

Serves: 6 / Preparation time: 10 minutes / Cooking time: 25 minutes

1 pound chicken breasts
1 can of pineapple chunks, about 20-ounce, drained
1 can of chopped green chilies, about 4.5-ounce
1 can of black beans, about 15-ounce, drained
1 medium white onion, peeled, diced
1 cup rice, cooked
1 teaspoon Jamaican jerk blend seasoning
1 tablespoon olive oil
1/2 cup jerk marinade

- Prepare the chicken and for this, cut it into 1-inch pieces and then season with jerk seasoning.
- Place a large skillet pan, place it over medium heat, add oil and when hot, add chicken pieces and cook for 5 minutes until brown on all sides.
- Transfer chicken pieces to a plate, add onion into the pan, and cook for 5 minutes until soft.

- Return chicken pieces into the pan, add remaining ingredients except for rice, and stir until mixed.
- Switch heat to the high level, bring the mixture to a boil, then switch heat to the low level and simmer for 10 minutes until chicken has thoroughly cooked.
- Serve chicken over cooked rice.

Per Serving: Calories: 310; Total Fat: 4.5 g; Saturated Fat: 0.5 g; Protein: 20 g; Carbs: 4.5 g; Fiber: 7 g; Sugar: 27 g

Peachy Spareribs

Serves: 8 / Preparation time: 10 minutes / Cooking time: 6 hours and 30 minutes

4 pounds of pork spareribs, cut into eight pieces
1 can of sliced peaches, about 15.25 ounces, undrained
½ teaspoon minced garlic
1 teaspoon salt
1 teaspoon ground bell pepper
1/2 cup brown sugar
2 tablespoons cornstarch
1/4 cup white vinegar
1/4 cup ketchup
2 tablespoons soy sauce

2 tablespoons olive oil
2 tablespoons cold water
Cooked rice, for serving

- Place a large skillet pan, place it over medium heat, add oil and when hot, add ribs pieces in a single layer and cook for 5 to 10 minutes per side until nicely browned.
- Switch on a slow cooker, place ribs in it, then top with remaining ingredients except for rice, cornstarch, and water and cook for 6 hours at low heat setting until ribs have turned tender.
- When done, transfer peaches and pork to a serving plate and then keep warm.
- Remove fat from the cooking juices in the slow cooker, transfer cooking juices into a small pan and bring it to a boil over medium heat.
- Stir together cornstarch and water, add to the liquid in a saucepan, stir until smooth, bring it to a boil, and then cook for 2 minutes until thickened.
- Serve pork over cooked rice, drizzle with sauce and then serve.

Per Serving: Calories: 518; Total Fat: 32 g; Saturated Fat: 12 g; Protein: 31 g; Carbs: 24 g; Fiber: 0 g; Sugar: 22 g

Eggplant Cacciatore

Serves: 4 / Preparation time: 10 minutes / Cooking time: 18 minutes

1 large eggplant, about 1 ½ pounds
1 medium white onion, peeled, chopped
1 can of mushroom stems and pieces, about 8-ounce, drained
1 can of stewed tomatoes, about 14.5-ounce, no salt added
1/4 teaspoon salt
1 teaspoon dried basil
1/8 teaspoon ground black pepper
2 tablespoons olive oil
1/2 cup shredded mozzarella cheese

- Place a large skillet pan, place it over medium heat, add oil and when hot, add onion and cook for 5 minutes until soft.
- Meanwhile, prepare the eggplant, and for this, cut it into ¾-inch pieces.
- Add eggplant into the cooked onion, cook for 10 to 12 minutes until tender, and then add remaining ingredients except for cheese.
- Switch heat to the high level, bring the mixture to a boil, and then simmer for 5 minutes until thickened.

- When done, sprinkle cheese over eggplant, let it stand for 5 minutes until cheese melts, and then serve.

Per Serving: Calories: 200; Total Fat: 10 g; Saturated Fat: 3 g; Protein: 7 g; Carbs: 23 g; Fiber: 8 g; Sugar: 12 g

Five Can Soup

Serves: 8 / Preparation time: 10 minutes / Cooking time: 10 minutes

1 can of prepared chili with beans, about 15-ounces
1 can of diced tomatoes with green chili peppers, about 10-ounces
1 can of whole kernel corn, about 14-ounces
1 can of tomato soup, about 10-ounces
1 can of vegetable beef soup, about 10.75 ounces

- Place a medium saucepan, place it over medium-high heat, add all the ingredients in it and stir until mixed.
- Cook for 10 minutes until thoroughly heated and then serve.

Per Serving: Calories: 130; Total Fat: 4 g; Saturated Fat: 2 g; Protein: 6.3 g; Carbs: 20.2 g; Fiber: 4.2 g; Sugar: 3 g

Ham and Cheese Potato Casserole

Serves: 5 / Preparation time: 10 minutes / Cooking time: 20 minutes

1 ¼ cups cubed cooked ham
1 package of frozen O'Brien potatoes, about 28 ounces
1 can of condensed cream of celery soup, about 10.75 ounces, undiluted
¼ teaspoon ground black pepper
1 cup sour cream
¼ cup of water
½ package of Velveeta cheese, about 16 ounces, cubed

- Switch on the oven, then set it to 375 degrees F and let it preheat.
- Meanwhile, take a large bowl, pour in water, sour cream, soup, and black pepper and whisk until combined.
- Add ham, potatoes, and cheese and then stir until mixed.
- Take a baking dish, spoon potato mixture in it, spread it evenly, cover with foil and then bake for 40 minutes.
- Uncover the baking dish and then continue baking for 15 minutes until bubbly.

- When done, let casserole stand for 10 minutes and then serve.

Per Serving: Calories: 474; Total Fat: 26 g; Saturated Fat: 14 g; Protein: 20 g; Carbs: 36 g; Fiber: 4 g; Sugar: 7 g

Chicken Burrito Skillet

Serves: 6 / Preparation time: 10 minutes / Cooking time: 30 minutes

1 cup long-grain rice, uncooked
1 pound chicken breasts
1 can of black beans, each about 15 ounces, drained
1 medium tomato, chopped
1 can of diced tomatoes, 14.5 ounces, drained
3 green onions, chopped
1/2 teaspoon onion powder
1/2 teaspoon garlic powder
1/8 teaspoon salt
1 teaspoon ground cumin
1/8 teaspoon ground black pepper
1/2 teaspoon red chili powder
2 tablespoons olive oil, divided
2 1/2 cups chicken broth

1 cup shredded Mexican cheese blend

- Prepare the chicken and for this, cut it into 1 ½ inches pieces, place them in a bowl and then season with salt and black pepper.
- Place a large skillet pan, place it over medium heat, add 1 tablespoon oil and when hot, add seasoned chicken pieces and cook for 2 minutes per side until nicely browned.
- Remove browned chicken pieces from the pan, add remaining oil in it, switch heat to medium-high level and when hot, add rice and cook for 2 minutes until golden brown.
- Add diced tomatoes, beans, and all the seasoning, pour in the broth, and bring the mixture to a boil.
- Top with chicken pieces, don't stir and then simmer for 20 minutes until chicken is cooked and rice has turned tender, covering the pan.
- When done, remove the pan from heat, sprinkle with cheese, and let stand for 5 minutes until cheese has melted.
- Top with chopped tomatoes and green onions and then serve.

Per Serving: Calories: 403; Total Fat: 13 g; Saturated Fat: 4 g; Protein: 27 g; Carbs: 43 g; Fiber: 5 g; Sugar: 4 g

Empanada Beef Chili

Serves: 6 / Preparation time: 10 minutes / Cooking time: 1 hour and 30 minutes

1 can of black beans, about 15 ounces, drained
1 medium onion, peeled, chopped
1 can of chopped green chilies, about 4 ounces
1 can of sliced olives, about 2.25 ounces, drained
1 ½ pound beef chuck steak, boneless
3 tablespoons minced cilantro
1 tablespoon minced garlic
1/2 teaspoon salt
2 teaspoons ground chipotle pepper
1/2 teaspoon ground black pepper
2 teaspoons ground cinnamon
1/2 cup raisins
1 can of tomato paste, about 6 ounces
4 teaspoons olive oil, divided
2 1/2 cups beef broth

- Prepare the beef and for this, cut it into 3/4-inch pieces, place them in a bowl and then season with salt and black pepper.

- Take a Dutch oven, place it over medium heat, add 2 teaspoons oil and when hot, add beef pieces and cook for 3 to 4 minutes per side until brown.
- Transfer beef pieces to a plate, add remaining oil and when hot, add onion and cook for 5 minutes until tender.
- Stir in garlic, cook for 1 minute until fragrant, stir in cinnamon, chipotle pepper, and tomato paste and cook for 3 minutes.
- Add cilantro, chilies, and raisins, pour in the broth, return beef pieces into the pot and bring the mixture to a boil.
- Switch heat to medium-low level and simmer for 1 hour until beef has turned tender.
- Add olives and beans and then cook for 10 minutes, don't uncover the pot.
- Serve straight away.

Per Serving: Calories: 373; Total Fat: 16 g; Saturated Fat: 5 g; Protein: 29 g; Carbs: 30 g; Fiber: 6 g; Sugar: 11 g

Tuna Balls with Spaghetti

Serves: 4 / Preparation time: 10 minutes / Cooking time: 45 minutes

For The Tuna Balls:
2 cans of tuna chunks, packed in oil, each about 5.6-ounces, drained
1 medium white onion, peeled, chopped
1 slice of brown bread, toasted
1 teaspoon minced garlic
3 tablespoons flour
½ teaspoon salt
1 teaspoon ground black pepper
1 teaspoon dried oregano
2 teaspoons dried parsley
1 lemon, zested
1 egg
2 ounces of grated cheddar cheese
For The Tomato Sauce and Spaghetti:
10.5 ounces spaghetti, cooked
1 medium white onion, peeled, chopped
½ teaspoon salt
1 teaspoon ground black pepper
½ teaspoon sugar
3 tablespoons tomato puree

2 tablespoons olive oil·
17.6 ounces canned passata

- Prepare tuna balls, and for this, torn bread into pieces and add them into a food processor.
- Add onion, garlic, lemon zest, salt, black pepper, parsley, and cheese and then pulse for 1 to 2 minutes until chopped.
- Then add tuna and egg and continue blending for 1 to 2 minutes until well combined.
- Take a shallow dish, place flour in it, and then stir in oregano.
- Shape the tuna mixture into sixteen balls and then roll them into flour mixture until coated.
- Transfer coated tuna balls to a plate, cover loosely with a plastic wrap, and then refrigerate for 30 minutes.
- Meanwhile, prepare the sauce and for this, take a large frying pan, place it over medium heat, add oil and when hot, add the onion.
- Stir in salt and sugar, cook for 10 minutes until softened and then stir in black pepper.
- Stir in tomato puree, cook for 2 minutes, switch heat to medium-low level, stir in passata and simmer the sauce for 20 minutes.

- After 30 minutes, remove tuna balls from the refrigerator and fry them for 3 minutes per side until nicely browned.
- Divide cooked pasta among bowls, top with sauce and tuna balls, and then serve.

Per Serving: Calories: 678; Total Fat: 21 g; Saturated Fat: 5.5 g; Protein: 40 g; Carbs: 79 g; Fiber: 7.5 g; Sugar: 14 g

Pineapple Chicken Fajitas

Serves: 6 / Preparation time: 10 minutes / Cooking time: 15 minutes

1 ½ pounds chicken tenderloins
2 cups sliced red onion
2 cans of pineapple tidbits, unsweetened, each about 8 ounces, drained
1 large green pepper, cored, cut into 1/2-inch strips
1 teaspoon garlic powder
1 large sweet red pepper, cored, 1/2-inch sliced
1 tablespoon minced jalapeno pepper, deseeded
3/4 teaspoon salt
3 teaspoons red chili powder
2 teaspoons ground cumin

2 tablespoons honey
2 tablespoons lime juice
2 tablespoons coconut oil, melted
12 corn tortillas, warmed

- Switch on the oven, then set it to 425 degrees F and let it preheat.
- Take a large bowl, add salt, chili powder, cumin, and garlic in it, pour in coconut oil, and stir until combined.
- Cut chicken in half lengthwise, add into the seasoning mixture, toss until coated, add onion, pineapple, and all the peppers, drizzle with lime juice and honey and then toss until combined.
- Take two large sheet pans, spread chicken and vegetables evenly between them, and then roast for 10 minutes until cooked, rotating pans halfway.
- Then switch on the broiler and broil chicken and vegetables for 3 to 5 minutes until chicken is no longer pink and vegetables are nicely browned.
- Divide chicken and vegetables among tortillas and then serve.

Per Serving: Calories: 359; Total Fat: 8 g; Saturated Fat: 4 g; Protein: 31 g; Carbs: 45 g; Fiber: 6 g; Sugar: 19 g

Bean and Beef Chili

Serves: 6 / Preparation time: 10 minutes / Cooking time: 6 hours

2 cans of pinto beans, each about 15 ounces, drained
1 pound ground beef
2 cans of black beans, each about 15 ounces, drained
2 cans of diced tomatoes with mild green chilies, each about 14.5 ounces
1 large sweet onion, peeled, chopped
1 ½ tablespoon minced garlic
1/2 teaspoon salt
3 tablespoons red chili powder
2 teaspoons ground cumin
For Topping:
Sour cream as needed
1 red onion, peeled, chopped
Minced cilantro as needed

- Place a large skillet pan, place it over medium heat, and when hot, add beef and then cook for 5 to 8 minutes until meat is no longer pink.
- Drain the excess grease, transfer beef into a slow cooker, discard liquid of one diced tomato can, add

tomatoes into the slow cooker along with remaining ingredients, and then stir until mixed.

- Plugin the slow cooker, shut with the lid, and then cook for 6 to 8 hours at low heat setting until done.
- When done, mash the black beans until chili reaches to desired consistency and then ladle into bowls.
- Top chili with sour cream, onion, and cilantro and then serve.

Per Serving: Calories: 264; Total Fat: 9.6 g; Saturated Fat: 3 g; Protein: 16 g; Carbs: 34 g; Fiber: 8.4 g; Sugar: 4.2 g

Broccoli Chicken Casserole

Serves: 6 / Preparation time: 10 minutes / Cooking time: 30 minutes

1 cup frozen broccoli florets, thawed
2 cups of cooked chicken, in cubes
1 package of chicken stuffing mix, about 6 ounces
1 can of condensed broccoli cheese soup, about 10.75 ounces, undiluted
1 cup shredded cheddar cheese

- Switch on the oven, then set it to 350 degrees F and let it preheat.
- Meanwhile, prepare chicken stuffing mix as mentioned on the package by using 1 ½ cup of water.
- Then take a large bowl, place cubed chicken it in, add broccoli, pour in soup, and stir until just mixed.
- Take a baking dish, grease it with oil, spoon chicken mixture in it, top with prepared stuffing mix and then sprinkle with cheese.
- Cover the baking dish with foil, bake for 20 minutes, then uncover it and continue baking for 10 minutes until thoroughly hot.
- Serve straight away.

Per Serving: Calories: 315; Total Fat: 13 g; Saturated Fat: 6 g; Protein: 23 g; Carbs: 25 g; Fiber: 2 g; Sugar: 4 g

Thai Prawn Green Curry

Serves: 4 / Preparation time: 10 minutes / Cooking time: 12 minutes

14-ounces jumbo prawns, peeled, deveined
14-ounces canned edamame
10-ounces canned mushrooms

1 large white onion, peeled, quartered

5.3-ounces canned whole baby sweetcorn cobs

1 red chili, chopped

7-ounces sugar snap peas

14-ounces canned French beans

½ cup coriander leaves

8-ounces canned bamboo shoots

2 teaspoons minced garlic

2 teaspoons grated ginger

1 tablespoon basil leaves

3-ounces jarred Green Thai Curry Paste

1 tablespoon rapeseed oil

1 tablespoon Thai fish sauce

3 ¾ cup canned coconut milk, unsweetened

To serve:

2 red chili, sliced lengthways

1 lime

- Place onion into a food processor, add chili, coriander, garlic, ginger, and green curry paste and then pulse for 1 minute until smooth.
- Take a medium saucepan, place it over medium heat, add oil and when hot, add onion mixture, and cook for 3 minutes.
- Pour in coconut milk, bring it to a boil, add all the vegetables, stir until mixed and bring it to a boil.

- Add prawns, cook for 5 minutes until they turn pink, and then remove the saucepan from heat.
- Stir in fish sauce, coriander, and basil leaves, garnish with red chili and then drizzle with lime juice.
- Serve straight away.

Per Serving: Calories: 471; Total Fat: 26 g; Saturated Fat: 14 g; Protein: 31.8 g; Carbs: 22 g; Fiber: 11 g; Sugar: 11.2 g

DESSERT

Banana Split Fluff

Serves: 10 / Preparation time: 10 minutes / Cooking time: 0 minutes

3 medium bananas, peeled, cut into chunks
1 can of cherry pie filling, about 21 ounces
1 can of crushed pineapple, about 8 ounces, drained

1 can of condensed milk, about 14 ounces, sweetened
1/2 cup chopped nuts
1 carton of frozen whipped topping, 12 ounces, thawed

- Take a large bowl, pour in milk, and then beat in whipped topping until well blended.
- Add remaining ingredients and then fold until just mixed.

Per Serving: Calories: 374; Total Fat: 13 g; Saturated Fat: 8 g; Protein: 5 g; Carbs: 58 g; Fiber: 2 g; Sugar: 49 g

Pineapple Pretzel Fluff

Serves: 12 / Preparation time: 10 minutes / Cooking time: 7 minutes

1 cup crushed pretzels
1 can of crushed pineapple, about 20 ounces, unsweetened, drained
1 cup sugar, divided
1 package of cream cheese, about 8 ounces, softened
1/2 cup butter, unsalted, melted
1 carton of frozen whipped topping, about 12 ounces, thawed

- Switch on the oven, then set it to 400 degrees F and let it preheat.
- Take a medium bowl, add pretzels in it along with ½ cup sugar and melted butter, and stir until mixed.
- Spread the pretzel mixture into a 9-inch pan, bake for 7 minutes, and then cool it thoroughly onto a wire rack.
- Meanwhile, take a large bowl, place cream cheese in it, and then beat in sugar until creamy.
- Fold in whipped topping and pineapple, cover the bowl and then refrigerate for 1 hour or until required for serving.
- When the pretzel mixture has cooled, break it into small pieces and then fold into pineapple mixture.
- Serve straight away.

Per Serving: Calories: 334; Total Fat: 19 g; Saturated Fat: 13 g; Protein: 2 g; Carbs: 37 g; Fiber: 1 g; Sugar: 31 g

Cranberry and Raspberry Salad

Serves: 10 / Preparation time: 10 minutes / Cooking time: 20 minutes

2 packages of raspberry gelatin, about 3 ounces each
1 can of crushed pineapple, about 8 ounces, undrained

1 can of whole-berry cranberry sauce, about 14 ounces

1 cup boiling water

1 cup of orange juice

- Take a large bowl, add gelatin in it, stir in water until it dissolves, and then stir in pineapple, cranberry sauce, and orange juice.
- Pour the mixture into a ring mold greased with oil, cover loosely with plastic wrap and then refrigerate for a minimum of 4 hours until set.
- When done, unmold the salad onto a plate and then serve.

Per Serving: Calories: 155; Total Fat: 0 g; Saturated Fat: 0 g; Protein: 2 g; Carbs: 39 g; Fiber: 1 g; Sugar: 32 g

Cherry Crisp

Serves: 4 / Preparation time: 10 minutes / Cooking time: 4 minutes

1 cup all-purpose flour

1 can of cherry pie filling, about 21 ounces

1/2 cup chopped walnuts

3/4 teaspoon ground cinnamon

1/4 cup brown sugar

1/4 teaspoon ground allspice

1 teaspoon lemon juice

1/3 cup cold butter, unsalted, cubed

Vanilla ice cream as needed for serving

- Take a microwave-proof dish, place the pie filling it and then stir in lemon juice until mixed.
- Take a food processor, place flour in it, add allspice, cinnamon, sugar, and butter in it and then pulse for 1 minute or more until mixture resembles crumbs.
- Spread the mixture over pie filling, top with nuts, and then microwave for 4 minutes until bubbling.
- Serve cherry crisp with ice cream

Per Serving: Calories: 567; Total Fat: 24 g; Saturated Fat: 10 g; Protein: 8 g; Carbs: 81 g; Fiber: 3 g; Sugar: 50 g

Tropical Compote Dessert

Serves: 6 / Preparation time: 10 minutes / Cooking time: 2 hours and 15 minutes

1 medium banana, peeled, sliced

1 can of mandarin oranges, about 15 ounces, drained

1 jar of mixed tropical fruit, about 23.5 ounces
1 jar of maraschino cherries, about 6 ounces, drained
1 tablespoon ginger powder
1 jalapeno pepper, deseeded, chopped
1/4 cup sugar
1/4 teaspoon ground cinnamon
6 tablespoons shredded coconut, sweetened, toasted
6 round sponge cakes

- Reserve ¼ cup syrup of tropical fruit, then place fruit into a slow cooker and add pepper.
- Add sugar into the reserved syrup along with ginger and cinnamon, stir until combined, and then pour this mixture over tropical fruit.
- Shut with the lid and then cook for 2 hours at a low heat setting.
- Then add banana, oranges, and cherries, stir until mixed and cook for another 15 minutes.
- Divide cakes among six plates, top with cooked compote, sprinkle with shredded coconut, and then serve.

Per Serving: Calories: 257; Total Fat: 3 g; Saturated Fat: 2 g; Protein: 1 g; Carbs: 62 g; Fiber: 3 g; Sugar: 31 g

Frozen Fruit Cups

Serves: 18 / Preparation time: 10 minutes / Cooking time: 0 minutes

1 can of crushed pineapple, about 8 ounces, drained
1 package of cream cheese, about 8 ounces, softened
1/2 cup chopped pecans
1 jar of maraschino cherries, about 10 ounces, drained
1 can of mandarin oranges, about 11 ounces, drained
1/2 cup sugar
1 carton of frozen whipped topping, about 8 ounces, thawed

- Take a large bowl, place cream cheese in it, and then beat in sugar until fluffy.
- Cut nine cherries in half and then chop the remaining ones.
- Add chopped cherries, pecans, and pineapple into cream cheese and then fold in oranges and whipped topping.
- Take 18 silicone muffin cups, fill them evenly with fruit mixture and then garnish with cherry halves.
- Place muffins cups into the freezer and chill for 1 hour or more until firm.
- Serve straight away.

Per Serving: Calories: 162; Total Fat: 9 g; Saturated Fat: 5 g; Protein: 1 g; Carbs: 20 g; Fiber: 1 g; Sugar: 17 g

Ambrosia Fruit Salad

Serves: 6 / Preparation time: 10 minutes / Cooking time: 0 minutes

1 can pineapple chunks, about 8 ounces, unsweetened, drained
1 cup miniature marshmallows
1 cup of green grapes
1 cup red grapes, seedless
1/2 cup shredded coconut, sweetened
1 banana, peeled, sliced
1 can of fruit cocktail, about 8.25 ounces, drained
3/4 cup vanilla yogurt

- Take a large bowl, place all the ingredients in it, and then fold until mixed.
- Refrigerate the salad for 1 hour and then serve.

Per Serving: Calories: 191; Total Fat: 4 g; Saturated Fat: 3 g; Protein: 3 g; Carbs: 40 g; Fiber: 2 g; Sugar: 34 g

Fluffed Fruit Salad

Serves: 14 / Preparation time: 10 minutes / Cooking time: 0 minutes

1 can pineapple tidbits, about 20 ounces, unsweetened drained
1/2 teaspoon orange zest
1 can of whole-berry cranberry sauce, about 14 ounces
1/2 cup toasted pecan halves
1 can of mandarin oranges, about 11 ounces, drained
1 carton of frozen whipped topping, about 8 ounces, thawed

- Take a large bowl, place oranges and pineapple in it, and then pour in cranberry sauce.
- Add orange zest and whipped topping and fold until just mixed.
- Garnish salad with pecans and then serve.

Per Serving: Calories: 138; Total Fat: 5 g; Saturated Fat: 0 g; Protein: 1 g; Carbs: 23 g; Fiber: 0 g; Sugar: 0 g

Peach Crumble

Serves: 4 / Preparation time: 10 minutes / Cooking time: 30 minutes

3 tablespoons rolled oats
2 cans of peaches, each about 14.4 ounces, sliced, drained
7 ounces flour
3 tablespoons brown sugar
1 teaspoon ground cinnamon
3 tablespoons butter, unsalted softened

- Switch on the oven, then set it to 356 degrees F and let it preheat.
- Take a heatproof dish and then cover its bottom with peaches.
- Take a medium bowl, place remaining ingredients in it, and stir until crumbly mixture comes together.
- Sprinkle this mixture over peaches and then bake for 30 minutes until golden brown and bubbly.
- Serve peach crumble with cream.

Per Serving: Calories: 102.5; Total Fat: 2.7 g; Saturated Fat: 0.7 g; Protein: 2.2 g; Carbs: 18.1 g; Fiber: 2.6 g; Sugar: 4.3 g

Peaches with Lemon and Yoghurt

Serves: 4 / Preparation time: 5 minutes / Cooking time: 10 minutes

1 can of peach halves, about 14.4 ounces, liquid reserved
2 lemon, juiced
2 tablespoons brown sugar
1/8 teaspoon ground nutmeg
7 ounces Greek yogurt

- Reserve the syrup of peaches and then pat dry the peaches.
- Take a grill pan, place it over medium-high heat, and when hot, place peach halves on it and grill for 3 to 4 minutes per side.
- Meanwhile, take a large frying pan, place it over medium-high heat, add maple syrup and sugar and then cook until sugar starts to bubble.
- Then stir in nutmeg, add grilled peach halves cut-side down, switch heat to medium-low level and cook for 2 minutes until golden brown.
- Turn the peach halves, cook for another 2 minutes, then drizzle with lemon juice and simmer for 2 minutes.
- When done, divide peaches among plates, top with yogurt, and then serve.

Per Serving: Calories: 140; Total Fat: 6 g; Saturated Fat: 2 g; Protein: 4 g; Carbs: 20 g; Fiber: 0 g; Sugar: 17 g

Cherry Grunt

Serves: 10 / Preparation time: 10 minutes / Cooking time: 25 minutes

1 cup all-purpose flour
1 can of tart red cherries, about 16 ounces, pitted, undrained
1/8 teaspoon salt
3/4 cup sugar, divided
1 1/2 teaspoons baking powder
1/2 teaspoon vanilla extract, unsweetened
1/4 cup butter, unsalted, divided
1/3 cup milk
1 1/2 cup water

- Take a Dutch oven, place it over medium heat, add cherries along with its juice, add 2 tablespoons butter, ½ cup sugar, then pour in water and simmer the mixture for 5 minutes.
- Meanwhile, place flour in a food processor, add remaining sugar, salt, baking powder, and butter and

then pulse for 1 minute until the mixture resembles crumbs.

- Add vanilla, pour in the milk, and then pulse for 1 minute until smooth.
- When cherries have cooked, drop a spoonful of the flour mixture, cover with the lid and simmer for 20 minutes until dumplings have thoroughly cooked.
- Serve straight away.

Per Serving: Calories: 183; Total Fat: 5 g; Saturated Fat: 3 g; Protein: 2 g; Carbs: 34 g; Fiber: 1 g; Sugar: 24 g

Fruit Compote

Serves: 8 / Preparation time: 10 minutes / Cooking time: 45 minutes

1 can of pineapple chunks, about 20 ounces, undrained
2 packages of dried blueberries, each about 3.5 ounces
1/2 cup golden raisins
1 can of sliced peaches, about 15.25 ounces, undrained
1 can of mandarin oranges, about 11 ounces, undrained
4 strips of lemon zest
1 package of dried plums, about 18 ounces, pitted
1 cinnamon stick, about 3 inches

1 package of dried apricots, about 6 ounces
1 jar of maraschino cherries, about 10 ounces, drained

- Reserve the juice of oranges, peaches, and pineapple and then place these fruits in a bowl.
- Take a Dutch oven, place it over medium heat, add dried fruits, cinnamon, and lemon strips, pour in fruit juices, and then bring it to a boil.
- Switch heat to medium-low level and simmer for 30 minutes until dried fruits have turned tender.
- Add fruits and cherries and then continue simmering for 10 minutes until thoroughly warmed.
- Serve straight away.

Per Serving: Calories: 126; Total Fat: 0 g; Saturated Fat: 0 g; Protein: 1 g; Carbs: 31 g; Fiber: 2 g; Sugar: 22 g

Cheesecake Pumpkin Dessert

Serves: 12 / Preparation time: 10 minutes / Cooking time: 40 minutes

For the Crust:
3/4 cup graham cracker crumbs
1/4 teaspoon ground cinnamon
3/4 cup chopped walnuts and more for topping

1/4 cup sugar

1/4 teaspoon ground ginger

1/4 cup butter, melted

1/8 teaspoon ground cloves

For the Filling:

1 cup canned pumpkin

1/2 teaspoon ground cinnamon, divided

3/4 cup sugar

2 tablespoons chopped walnuts

2 packages of cream cheese, each about 8 ounces, softened

2 eggs, beaten

- Switch on the oven, then set it to 350 degrees F and let it preheat.
- Prepare the crust and for this, take a small bowl, place all the ingredients in it and then stir until well combined.
- Take a 9-inch tart pan with a removable bottom and then spread base mixture evenly in its bottom.
- Prepare the filling, and for this, take a large bowl, place cream cheese in it, and then beat in sugar until smooth.
- Beat in eggs, one at a time, until combined and then beat in ¼ teaspoon cinnamon and pumpkin until just mixed.
- Pour the mixture over crust, spread it evenly, sprinkle remaining cinnamon and some walnuts on top and then bake for 40 minutes until set.

- When done, cool the dessert on the wire rack, cut it into slices and then serve.

Per Serving: Calories: 327; Total Fat: 24 g; Saturated Fat: 11 g; Protein: 7 g; Carbs: 25 g; Fiber: 2 g; Sugar: 19 g

Coconut Dessert Fluff Salad

Serves: 2 / Preparation time: 10 minutes / Cooking time: 0 minutes

2 cans of any fruit, each about 15 ounces, drained
1/4 cup coconut flakes, unsweetened
1 tablespoon maple syrup
1 teaspoon vanilla extract, unsweetened
2 cans of coconut milk, about 13.5 ounces, chilled

- Open the cans of milk, then separate solid and liquid parts and transfer solid part into a medium bowl.
- Add vanilla and maple syrup in it and then whisk well by using an immersion blender until smooth.
- Add drained fruits, sprinkle with coconut flakes and then fold until just mixed.
- Refrigerate salad for 30 minutes and then serve.

Per Serving: Calories: 440; Total Fat: 31 g; Saturated Fat: 27 g; Protein: 4 g; Carbs: 43 g; Fiber: 1 g; Sugar: 35 g

BEVERAGES

Mango, Peach and Banana Smoothie

Serves: 2 / Preparation time: 5 minutes / Cooking time: 0 minutes

2 ounces canned mango slices, packed in light syrup, drained
2 tablespoons oats
2 ounces canned peach slices, packed in juice, drained
1 frozen banana, peeled
½ teaspoon ground cinnamon
¼ teaspoon vanilla extract, unsweetened
1 tablespoon grated coconut
1 1/3 cup milk
½ cup ice cubes

- Add all the ingredients in the order into a food processor or blender and then pulse for 1 minute or more until smooth.
- Pour smoothie into glasses and then serve.

Per Serving: Calories: 260; Total Fat: 8.5 g; Saturated Fat: 6 g; Protein: 8.5 g; Carbs: 35 g; Fiber: 4 g; Sugar: 23 g

Banana and Mango Smoothie

Serves: 2 / Preparation time: 5 minutes / Cooking time: 0 minutes

1 can of diced mango, about 15-ounces, drained
1 large frozen banana, peeled
¼ teaspoon vanilla extract, unsweetened
1 teaspoon honey
2/3 cup canned coconut milk, unsweetened

- Add all the ingredients in the order into a food processor or blender and then pulse for 1 minute or more until smooth.
- Pour smoothie into glasses and then serve.

Per Serving: Calories: 160; Total Fat: 0.7 g; Saturated Fat: 0.3 g; Protein: 5.1 g; Carbs: 36.1 g; Fiber: 2.6 g; Sugar: 3 g

Cranberry Orange Smoothie

Serves: 4 / Preparation time: 5 minutes / Cooking time: 0 minutes

1 can of mandarin oranges in juice, about 11-ounce, drained
1/8 teaspoon salt
1/8 teaspoon ground cinnamon
1 teaspoon vanilla extract, unsweetened
2 tablespoons maple syrup
2½ cups Greek yogurt
1 can of whole cranberry sauce, about 14-ounce

- Add all the ingredients in the order into a food processor or blender and then pulse for 1 minute or more until smooth.
- Pour smoothie into glasses and then serve.

Per Serving: Calories: 303; Total Fat: 3 g; Saturated Fat: 2 g; Protein: 13 g; Carbs: 58 g; Fiber: 2 g; Sugar: 56 g

Mango and Ginger Smoothie

Serves: 2 / Preparation time: 5 minutes / Cooking time: 0 minutes

1 can of diced mango, about 15-ounces, drained
1/2 can of evaporated milk, about 12-ounces
1 tablespoon minced ginger
1 tablespoon honey
1 cup of ice cubes

- Add all the ingredients in the order into a food processor or blender and then pulse for 1 minute or more until smooth.
- Pour smoothie into glasses and then serve.

Per Serving: Calories: 371; Total Fat: 7 g; Saturated Fat: 2 g; Protein: 7 g; Carbs: 64 g; Fiber: 2 g; Sugar: 61 g

Tropical Smoothie

Serves: 2 / Preparation time: 5 minutes / Cooking time: 0 minutes

2 frozen bananas, sliced
1 cup of frozen mango
1 cup frozen pineapple
1/2 cup canned coconut milk, unsweetened
3/4 cup pineapple juice

- Add all the ingredients in the order into a food processor or blender and then pulse for 1 minute or more until smooth.
- Pour smoothie into glasses and then serve.

Per Serving: Calories: 315; Total Fat: 12 g; Saturated Fat: 10 g; Protein: 2 g; Carbs: 49 g; Fiber: 4 g; Sugar: 37 g

Intense Fruit Smoothie

Serves: 2 / Preparation time: 5 minutes / Cooking time: 0 minutes

1 package of frozen mixed berries, about 10-ounces
1 can of sliced peaches, about 15 ounces, drained
2 tablespoons honey

- Add all the ingredients in the order into a food processor or blender and then pulse for 1 minute or more until smooth.
- Pour smoothie into glasses and then serve.

Per Serving: Calories: 293; Total Fat: 0.3 g; Saturated Fat: 0 g; Protein: 3.4 g; Carbs: 75.5 g; Fiber: 5.4 g; Sugar: 39 g

Peach, Berries and Yogurt Smoothie

Serves: 2 / Preparation time: 5 minutes / Cooking time: 0 minutes

1 can of Sliced Peaches, packed in Syrup, about 15.25 ounces, undrained
½ cup frozen raspberries
2/3 cup Greek yogurt
½ cup of ice cubes

- Add all the ingredients in the order into a food processor or blender and then pulse for 1 minute or more until smooth.
- Pour smoothie into glasses and then serve.

Per Serving: Calories: 150; Total Fat: 2.5 g; Saturated Fat: 1.5 g; Protein: 5 g; Carbs: 28 g; Fiber: 4 g; Sugar: 22 g

Pumpkin Smoothie

Serves: 4 / Preparation time: 5 minutes / Cooking time: 0 minutes

1 tablespoon ground flaxseed

1 frozen banana, peeled

1/4 teaspoon cinnamon

1/4 teaspoon pumpkin pie spice

1 tablespoon honey

1/3 cup pumpkin puree

1 cup of vanilla soy milk

- Add all the ingredients in the order into a food processor or blender and then pulse for 1 minute or more until smooth.
- Pour smoothie into a glass and then serve.

Per Serving: Calories: 196.6; Total Fat: 2 g; Saturated Fat: 0.2 g; Protein: 14.2 g; Carbs: 33.4 g; Fiber: 6.2 g; Sugar: 20 g

Raspberry and Apricot Smoothie Bowl

Serves: 4 / Preparation time: 5 minutes / Cooking time: 0 minutes

3 tablespoons porridge oats

10.5 ounces of canned raspberries, drained

10.5 ounces of canned apricots, drained

1 tablespoon flaked almonds

2 tablespoons pumpkin seeds
10.5 ounces of Greek yogurt

- Add berries, oats, and yogurt into a food processor or blender and then pulse for 1 minute or more until smooth.
- Divide smoothie between four bowls, top with apricots and remaining ingredients, and then serve.

Per Serving: Calories: 406; Total Fat: 17.3 g; Saturated Fat: 3.7 g; Protein: 25.1 g; Carbs: 35.5 g; Fiber: 3.9 g; Sugar: 17.6 g

Pumpkin Banana Smoothie

Serves: 1 / Preparation time: 5 minutes / Cooking time: 0 minutes

1 frozen banana, peeled
2 tablespoons canned pumpkin
1/8 teaspoon nutmeg
1/8 teaspoon cinnamon
1/2 teaspoon honey
2 tablespoons Greek yogurt
5 tablespoons milk, unsweetened
1/4 cup ice cubes

- Add all the ingredients in the order into a food processor or blender and then pulse for 1 minute or more until smooth.
- Pour smoothie into a glass and then serve.

Per Serving: Calories: 189; Total Fat: 3.03 g; Saturated Fat: 1.6 g; Protein: 7.06 g; Carbs: 37.1 g; Fiber: 3.9 g; Sugar: 23.06 g

Manufactured by Amazon.ca
Bolton, ON